THE CHAMPIONS

Tom Seaver
Joe Namath
Johnny Bench
Bobby Orr
Vida Blue
Pete Maravich
Bob Griese
Willis Reed
Brooks Robinson
Bobby Hull
Johnny Unitas
Kareem Jabbar
Phil Esposito
Leroy Kelly
Roberto Clemente
Dick Butkus
Bob Gibson
Merlin Olsen
Gale Sayers
Gordie Howe
Gene Washington
Lem Barney
Rick Barry
Jacques Plante
Lance Alworth
Hank Aaron
Oscar Robertson
Carl Yastrzemski
Jerry West
Willie Mays

THE CHAMPIONS

By Bernard Garfinkel

Illustrations by David K. Stone

Photographs by Dan Baliotti

Platt & Munk,

Publishers/New York

For two other champions,
Peter and David Franck

Prepared and produced for the publisher by BMG Productions, Incorporated.

Published in New York by Platt & Munk.
Library of Congress Catalog Card Number 70-185971.

CONTENTS

Joe Namath

Joe Namath sat on the sidelines in Shea Stadium on November 28, 1971, watching the Jets in action against the San Francisco 49ers. It was an occupation he had become accustomed to but didn't like. He had not played in a regular season game since the beginning of the 1970 season, 19 games before, when he broke his wrist in the Jets' fifth game against the Baltimore Colts.

Namath had started out the 1971 season hoping to come back strong. But in the Jets' very first exhibition game, against the Detroit Lions, with Namath looking sharp as he passed and directed the team, disaster struck again. Detroit linebacker Mike Lucci intercepted a pass and Namath found himself between Lucci and the goal line. He might have played it safe. It was, after all, just an exhibition game. But Namath has a football player's instincts. He was in the game and he had to take his shot. He tried tackling Lucci, was hit by another Detroit player and tore the cartilage in his left knee.

That required an operation. The knee had healed well but at this point Namath was still rusty, 15 pounds underweight and with just two weeks of solid practice under his belt. So he sat on the sidelines and watched reserve quarterback Bob Davis run the team.

The 49ers were ahead 7-0 with five minutes left in the first quarter when Davis was hit and limped off the field with a sprained ankle. The crowd of 64,000 cheered. Namath was coming in.

The cheers weren't wasted. Namath was not at the top of his form. Some of his passes were wobbly. His timing was off. But he completed 11 out of 27 passes, three of them for touchdowns, against the team with the best defensive statistics in the National Football Conference.

Coming into the game's final minute, Namath brought the Jets down to the 49ers' 19-yard line. But his final pass was intercepted and the 49ers held on for a 24-21 victory. Still, Namath's per-formance was the best thing that had happened to the Jets in a year.

Joe Namath has always risen to occasions as a football player. It is this quality, as much as his ability to throw a ball exceptionally well, that makes him the great quarterback he is. Namath is an inspirational team leader. He was in college, he is with the Jets. Tackle Winston Hill reflects the Jets' feeling about Namath when he says: "Make no mistake about it, he's the best, past, present, possibly future."

Namath's performance against the 49ers was reminiscent of his last game for the University of Alabama in the Orange Bowl on New Year's Day, 1965. Namath had injured his right knee during the season. He went on playing, knowing he would need an operation after the season had ended. Just before the Orange Bowl, his leg collapsed. It was doubtful that he'd be able to play in the Bowl. But with Alabama trailing Texas by two touchdowns in the second quarter, Namath came into the game, limping, wearing a leg brace. He completed 18 of 27 passes for two touchdowns and as the game ended with Texas leading 21-17, he brought Alabama on a drive to within inches of the Texas goal line.

Namath came to Alabama from Beaver Falls High School in Beaver Falls, Pennsylvania. A gifted athlete, he starred in baseball and basketball as well as football. The Kansas City baseball club offered him a $15,000 bonus to sign, but Namath's first love was football, and he wanted a college education besides.

As Alabama's quarterback, Namath led the team to a three-year, 29-4 record, and Alabama coach Bear Bryant called him "the greatest athlete I have ever coached."

Bryant's opinion of Namath was confirmed and expanded upon in the Jets scouting report on him: "An outstanding passer with big good hands and

Namath excels in spotting open receivers.

He was, in truth, a crippled ballplayer who somehow managed to play anyway.

Bad knees and all, Namath came into his own in 1967, passing for a new pro football record of more than 4000 yards in one season as the Jets were in the thick of the fight for the title with an 8-5-1 record.

Then came 1968, the Jets' Cinderella year. They took the eastern division title with an 11-3 record, then played the Oakland Raiders, the western division champions, who had beaten them earlier in the year. The winner would go to the Super Bowl.

In a marvelously exciting football game, the Jets led in the middle of the fourth quarter, 20-16, on two Namath touchdown passes and two field goals. Oakland intercepted a Namath pass intended for Maynard, and scored one play later on a run to take the lead 23-20. Namath came right back in a brilliant display. A ten-yard pass to Sauer, a 52-yard pass to Maynard and the Jets were on Oakland's six. On the next play Namath faked to Snell and hit Maynard in the end zone to make the score 26-23. Two desperate Oakland drives failed and the Jets were in the Super Bowl.

The Jets were established as 18 point underdogs. A strong defensive team, Baltimore had a 15-1 record. In only five of its games had the Colts let the opposition score more than one touchdown. The game would boil down to the Colts' defense versus Namath, the brilliant quarterback. The odds didn't faze Namath. He calmly announced that the Jets would beat the Colts.

In one of the great upsets in sports, they did. The score was 16-7, and the Jet victory was a convincing one. The Jet defense throttled the passing of Earl Morrall and Johnny Unitas while the Jet offense took advantage of its opportunities. Namath drew first blood by engineering an 80-yard drive in the second quarter, mixing runs and passes, and sending Matt Snell over from the four yard line. The other Jet scores came on field goals by Jim Turner. Baltimore's only score came late in the game, after Johnny Unitas had replaced Morrall.

In the locker room after the game, Joe Namath's father embraced his son and said: "I told them you could do it." So had Joe, and now they believed him.

exceptionally fast delivery. Has good agility and sets up very well. Throws the short pass very well and can also throw the bomb with great accuracy. Is smart and follows the game plan perfectly. Is a fine leader, and the team has great confidence in him."

Namath got a reported $400,000 to sign with the Jets. The Jet owners felt that he would not only be a great player but a crowd-pleaser as well.

With Namath as the key man and players like Matt Snell, George Sauer, Don Maynard and Emerson Boozer, the Jets slowly began to work their way up in the standings. In 1965, Namath was Rookie of the Year and the Jets were 5-8. In 1966, Namath and the Jets were up and down, and the team finished with a 6-6 record.

Meanwhile, Namath had to contend with his knees. In 1965, he had an operation on the right knee to repair damaged cartilage. In 1966, he developed tendinitis in the left knee because he had been favoring the right one, and he had to have another operation on the right one as well.

Vida Blue

Yankee outfielder Roy White thinks "it speeds up on you and then seems to disappear." Paul Schaal, Kansas City Royals third baseman, says that it "jumps right over your bat." Los Angeles Dodgers outfielder Frank Robinson says "it tails away from you and sometimes it doesn't."

What they're all talking about, of course, is what has become America's most celebrated pitch, the fastball thrown by Vida Rochelle Blue, Jr. of the Oakland Athletics. Blue himself says that his fastball "can go straight, sail or sink." Whatever it does exactly, there's no doubt that it's a potent pitch, so potent that it gave Vida Blue a 24-8 record, 301 strikeouts and the league's lowest earned run average, 1.82 for 312 innings. For compiling those statistics, Blue was named the American League's Most Valuable Player in 1971 and at 22 became the youngest player ever to win the Cy Young award as the year's outstanding pitcher.

Vida Blue's story is so much like the favorite fantasy of every baseball-loving American boy that it sometimes seems unreal, a Hollywood fairy tale that could never happen in actuality. He was born and grew up in Mansfield, Louisiana, a town of 6,300 people in the northwestern part of the state. His father worked in the local iron foundry. Vida was the oldest; there were five other children. "A natural," Vida loved playing ball and spent all of his spare time tossing baseballs and footballs on a vacant lot across the street from the Blue's eight-room house. "In the summer," Vida says, "you'd just get up and eat and play ball, then come back and eat and play ball some more."

By the time he was in junior high and playing Little League baseball, there was no one around who could consistently catch his fastball. Vida entered DeSoto High School in September 1964 as a sophomore. In anticipation of his coming, the school organized a baseball team for the first time, the diamond laid out on a corner of the football field, with the football lights cutting across the outfield.

Blue was six feet when he entered high school, big enough to play football, and he was as devastating on a football field as on a diamond. He threw mainly left-handed but on occasion he threw right-handed as well, and he could launch 50 and 60 yard bullets with ease. His shorter passes, says DeSoto coach Clarence Baldwin, sometimes "knocked the receiver right down." In his senior year, Blue threw 35 touchdown passes in 14 games. He was also the team's best runner.

Football was his first love, in fact, and he dreamed of playing quarterback on the Baltimore Colts. He might well have been professional football's first black quarterback. But when his father died, just as scholarship offers came from more than two dozen colleges, including Notre Dame, Purdue and the University of Houston, Blue had to make a hard decision. He was 17, the oldest child; there was very little money.

Then Kansas City scout Connie Ryan saw him pitch in Mansfield (Kansas City moved to Oakland in 1967). Ryan offered him a bonus, reported to be $35,000, after telling owner Charles Finley: "He is the best lefthander I have seen in nine years of scouting."

Blue was in no position to turn down that amount, so he signed. In the fall of 1967 he reported to the Arizona Instructional League in Mesa, where he played in two games. After spring training in 1968, he was assigned to the Burlington Iowa Bees, a Class A team.

At Burlington and in 1969 at Birmingham, a notch closer to the majors, Blue worked on developing a curve and change-up. He pitched regularly and, overall, fairly well and was called up to Oakland in July 1969.

In his first crack at the major leagues, Vida Blue was not a smashing success. He started four games and ended up with a 1-1 record. Used in relief he pitched just 42 innings, gave up 49 hits, 34 runs, 18 walks and had an earned run average of 6.21. Hardly a Cy Young performance.

The problem, Blue himself knew well, was he had just one really effective pitch. He needed a curve and change-up to go with his fastball.

Before the season ended, he was called up for six months of military duty, and at camp, pitching to a minor league catcher there, he felt that he made a good deal of progress on his change-up.

When he reported for spring training at Mesa in 1970, he told the veteran pitcher Juan Pizzaro about his trouble controlling a curve. Pizzaro showed him a new grip and Blue found that using it he could control the curve far better than before.

Now he had three pitches and when he was sent to the Iowa Oaks at Des Moines, a Class AAA club, the improvement showed up immediately. In his first start, he won 7-1, striking out 14 in seven innings. By the end of May he had six straight wins and he continued to notch victories until the beginning of August, when he was called up to Oakland again, only to be sent back down after just 11 days.

When the American Association season was over on September 3, Vida Blue was called up to Oakland again. This time he was there to stay.

He pitched four innings against the Chicago White Sox and hit a game-winning home run, beat Kansas City 3-0 on a one-hitter. Then, against the Minnesota Twins, Vida Blue came into his own. Pitching against Jim Perry, who'd beaten the A's 12 straight times in a span of time going back to 1966, Blue fired a no-hitter, the fourth of the major league season.

For Vida Blue, the no-hitter was proof enough that he had what it takes to pitch major league baseball. Even after he lost the opening game of the 1971 season to Washington, his confidence was undiminished. In the locker room after the game, Charlie Finley asked Blue about the two dimes he had carried in his hip pocket. "Twenty cents, twenty games," Blue replied.

He made it with four to spare, in one of the most phenomenal pitching exhibitions in the major leagues. By the All-Star game in July, Blue had won 17 games, averaging more than a strikeout an inning. He shut out Kansas City 5-0 for his first victory in a rain-shortened six-inning game, striking out 13, beat the Milwaukee Brewers 2-0 on two hits, beat the White Sox 11-2, the Angels 7-3, the Orioles 1-0, the Indians 3-1, the Tigers 5-0, the Orioles again 2-1, the Brewers 3-0, the Twins 3-1. Ten victories, ten complete games and he was leading the American League in victories, strikeouts and earned run average.

Fans flocked to see him and it was estimated that when he pitched he brought 15,000 extra people into the ball park. Newspaper and magazine reporters hounded him for stories. And he went on winning. By the middle of August his record was 21-4, with 240 strikeouts, 8 shutouts and a 1.62 earned run average. In the last half of the season, Blue lost five tough games in which the A's scored just three runs for him, and ended up with the 24-8 record that could as easily have been 29-3.

Through it all, Blue was under enormous pressure yet remained what he essentially is, a modest, clean-living 22-year-old with great talent and a lot of poise. Asked by Charlie Finley to change his name to Vida True Blue (so that Vida could be dropped and he'd be known as True Blue), he refused. "Vida was my father's name," he said, "and every time I pitch I honor him."

Having led Oakland to the West championship, Blue was disappointed when he lost the first game of the playoffs against Baltimore and then watched Oakland lose two more as Baltimore moved on to the World Series against the Pirates.

He was even more disappointed in the spring when he and Charlie Finley squared off against each other in a salary squabble. It was not settled until the beginning of May, and Blue missed all of spring training and a couple of months of the season.

Now Blue is again ready to do what he does best — make his fastball "jump over a few bats." His pitching philosophy is simple and straightforward: "My high school coach," he says, "used to tell me, 'Small fish don't swim in deep water.' To be a winner, you have to want to be the biggest fish there is, you have to want to be the best."

■

Bobby Hull

The golden hair has gone on top now, but the superlative body is still intact: the body of a well-conditioned heavyweight, the muscles hard and bulging. When he starts his sixteenth season in the NHL in the fall of 1972, the Chicago Black Hawks' Golden Jet, Bobby Hull, will still be the game's most exciting player, the leading scorer of his time, the crowd-pleasing hockey machine whose solo dashes down the ice—great legs pumping, massive shoulders bobbing up and back—never fail to draw an anticipating wail of pleasure from the excitement-eager crowd.

In the excellence of his play and in his achievements in the rink, Hull ranks at the very top level, alongside of the legendary Maurice "The Rocket" Richard, Gordie Howe and Bobby Orr. Of these, only Richard had an equivalent capacity to excite the fans, and Richard never had the adoring army of supporters that Hull has.

Near the end of the 1972 season, in a game against the Boston Bruins in Boston Garden on March 25, Hull scored his 600th goal. (Only Howe has scored more: 786 over 25 seasons.) The Boston fans rose to give him a roaring, 30-second ovation. It was reminiscent of a previous ovation Hull received. That came on March 12, 1965. Chicago playing New York in the Chicago arena. At 4:34 of the third period, Hull got the puck in center ice. He started toward the Ranger goal and, as a Ranger defenseman came toward him, he slapped his shot from 50 feet out. The puck came in low and to the right. The Ranger goalie, Cesare Maniago, stuck out his stick but missed the puck.

As the red light went on, the Chicago fans began to cheer. The wild ovation lasted for seven and a half minutes. Hull had broken what seemed to be the unattainable record in hockey, a record comparable to Babe Ruth's mark of 60 home runs. He had broken Maurice Richard's mark by scoring

his 51st goal of the season. Hull went on to score three more goals that year, and his total of 54 goals still stands as a supreme achievement, for after that the league added new teams and increased the number of games on the schedule. Scoring became easier and Hull himself broke his own mark during the 1968-69 season when he made 58 goals. Since then, Phil Esposito has gone over 70 and it is likely that a 80-goal season will be registered in the next few years.

Bobby Hull has kept pace with the new scoring spree. He's the only man ever to have scored more than 50 goals in four NHL seasons. Among other records, he has scored 30 or more goals in the last 13 seasons and 40 or more in the last eight. But it's not just Hull's potent scoring punch that delights fans. It's the way he plays the game, and the way he plays the game is based on his enormous strength.

Hull was born in 1939 in Point Anne, Ontario, one of 11 children. At seven, he could lift his 210-pound father off the floor on his back. He developed that natural strength by chopping trees in the nearby woods and shoveling snow in the winter. He started skating when he was three, began playing organized hockey at ten, and was signed in the junior hockey league by the Black Hawks when he was 13.

When he came up to the NHL in 1957, Hull was what could be called "an imposing specimen." At 5'10" he weighed 190 pounds, had a 44-inch chest that tapered down to a 32-inch waist, muscular thighs and legs that were like proverbial oak trees. Because of his leg strength, particularly, Hull has great skating speed—he's been timed at 30 miles an hour on the ice.

With his powerful slap shot, which comes whistling in like a projectile from amazing distances, and his great skating speed, Hull is like a fast-

Hull *(center)*, has fastest shot in hockey, clocked at more than 100 miles per hour.

moving cannon on the ice. And what he likes best of all is the break-away solo shot. He'll start at his own end of the ice and, using his speed and power, either out-race and outmaneuver defensemen or simply bust through two or three who try to stop him. Goaltenders around the league have special Bobby Hull nightmares. They talk about his power, speed, unstoppable shots—and with good reason. In one game against Toronto, Hull let fly a shot against goalie Johnny Bower that knocked him cold. Bower was replaced by Terry Sawchuk and a few minutes later Sawchuk too was flat on his back, unconscious from another Hull shot.

On the ice, Hull is respected for his sportsmanlike behavior. And of all the men playing today, he probably has more right than any other to play rough, for no one has taken more punishment than Hull. In 1965, for example, he won the Lady Byng Trophy for sportsmanlike conduct, because that was the year other teams decided the way to stop him was to knock him down. Hull shrugged off the rough treatment and kept barreling through. Most teams assign a "shadow" to trail Hull throughout a game. The shadow's job is to keep him away

from the action. Some do it by fair means, others by foul, and Hull's battered face is eloquent testimony to the beatings he's taken. "I must have put at least 200 stitches in this guy myself, since he joined the club," says Nick Garen, the Black Hawks' trainer. Given enough provocation, a really flagrant foul, Hull will fight back, but for the most part, he takes his punishment and plows ahead.

Hull has changed his game somewhat, however, mainly at the direction of Chicago coach Billy Ray. He's playing a more defensive game now, staying in his territory, checking his man instead of chasing the puck all over the ring as he used to.

And still he remains the deadly scoring threat. In a 1972 game against the Rangers, for instance, Hull got the puck from teammate Pit Martin in a faceoff near the Ranger goal. The puck came at him, Hull flashed his stick at it and the puck went sailing off on a low line toward the goal 25 feet away. Ranger goalie Ed Giacomin pushed a leg out to stop it—too late.

"You can't lose the puck to Hull at that spot," Emile Francis, the Ranger coach, said later. "There's no one in the league who gets it away faster."

Gale Sayers

The word "rookie" isn't normally tossed around as a term of praise. Veteran athletes, in fact, use it to put down newcomers, and the "rook" in training camp and during his first year with a team normally takes a fair amount of kidding, if not more serious punishment. One rookie who turned the word inside out, however, was a 6', 200-pound graduate of the University of Kansas who came to play with the Chicago Bears because, as he said, "I want to play with the best and against the best." For that reason, he had turned down a lot more money from Kansas City in the AFL to sign a three-year $150,000 contract with Chicago. This is an amount not to be sneered at, of course, and an indication that this rookie was out of the ordinary.

Gale Sayers had come out of the University of Kansas as one of the best running backs in the country, powerful, fast and shifty, averaging over six yards a carry, shattering conference records and making most All-America teams in his junior and senior years.

Born in Wichita, Kansas, Sayers grew up in Omaha, Nebraska, where he was a spectacular all-state running back at Omaha Central High School. Considering numerous college offers, he decided on Kansas because he liked the coach, because it was close to home and because it had a good football team. His aim was to play pro ball, and he wanted to be noticed in college.

Just how out of the ordinary Sayers really was didn't become apparent until the third game of the 1965 season. There had been, to begin with, trouble at the College All-Star training camp. What the problem was exactly is not clear. One version is that Sayers and the All-Stars' coach Otto Graham had a "personality clash." Another is that Sayers hurt his leg at the start of the camp, but the doctors and Graham didn't believe there was any-

thing wrong with the leg. In any event, Sayers did not play in the game. He refuses to explain what happened, but he does say: "I was hurt."

Whether or not the incident affected his performance when he got to the Bears, he started slowly. He did get into a few exhibition games, and there were hints of the fireworks he could provide. Against the Los Angeles Rams, he returned a punt 77 yards for a touchdown and uncorked a 93-yard kickoff return. But when the regular season started, Sayers was sitting on the bench, and in the first two games he carried the ball just twice.

In the Bears' third game, Sayers, as one reporter said, "burst from his rookie cocoon." Packers-Bears games are, traditionally, all-out affairs, each team regarding the other as its most cherished enemy.

In 1965, under Vince Lombardi, the Packers were riding high, having won two league and three division championships in the past five years. The Bears, on the other hand, were in the middle of much leaner days. Their league championship in 1963 was their first taste of glory in 10 years. Green Bay lived up to its recent past by beating the Bears. But in the second half, the Chicago team looked good, outscoring the Packers 14-3 and rolling up 309 yards. And Sayers had his first big day, with a 65-yard pass reception, a six yard touchdown run and a total of five catches and 80 yards rushing in 17 carries.

Now Sayers was in the starting line-up, and for the rest of the season there was no stopping him. He put together game after sensational game, scampering across yard stripes like a man who thought he was at a track meet.

The Bears next game was against the Los Angeles Rams. In this one, Sayers went 80 yards with a screen pass, shaking off two Rams along the way, one of whom was riding on his back for a while. Bring on the Minnesota Vikings, whose coach, Norm Van Brocklin had been heard to say that Sayers wasn't much. He probably shouldn't have been heard saying that. The score was 37-31, favor of the Vikings, with two minutes to go when Sayers apparently started concentrating on hating Van Brocklin. Earlier in the game, his attention must have been wandering. All he had done was score two touchdowns on receptions of 18 and 25 yards. Now the Vikings kicked off to Chicago. Sayers took the ball on the goal line and headed up the left side like a runaway greyhound to score. For good measure, moments later, after Chicago had intercepted a Viking pass, he went over for another touchdown from the 11-yard line.

Against Green Bay in Chicago, he ran a kick back 62 yards and scored on a 10-yard run. Against the Giants, he ran 45 yards for one touchdown, 15 for another, gaining 113 yards on 13 carries, the first time he had broken the 100-yard mark. Now reporters were calling Sayers "the marvelously exciting running back," and asking Bears' coach George Halas the secrets of his success.

"He has wonderful speed," Halas said, "and he has tremendous acceleration and a variety of gears. He can lull you into thinking he is going at top speed, and then turn up another notch and be gone before you know it."

That was a fair description of what Sayers did to the Giants on his first touchdown run. Swinging wide to his left, he turned upfield, faked a pass — which stopped a Giant linebacker long enough for a Bear to take him out of the play — and once past the linebacker, put on speed to breeze by a band of Giant defenders.

More razzle-dazzle in the Baltimore game, in which he picked up 118 yards rushing, including a 61-yard run on which he eluded a Baltimore cornerback with a beautifully executed inside-outside-inside body swivel that left the Colt grabbing air.

Sayers put the whipped cream on all this cake in the next-to-the-last game of the season, against the San Francisco 49ers in Chicago's Wrigley Field. The field was muddy from rain, not a runner's field—except for Sayers. On the first play he went 80 yards on a screen pass for a TD. He scored two more touchdowns in the first half, one on a run of 21 yards, the other of seven. In the second half, he scored on a one-yard buck and a 50-yard run. And finally, in the fourth period, he gathered in a punt on the 15 yard line, went straight upfield, cut to his right and flashed away. Crossing the goal line, he flipped the ball in the air and clapped his hands, then danced back to his teammates on the sidelines. It was a large display of emotion for the usually reserved Sayers.

Ernie Nevers, the only other man who ever scored six touchdowns in an NFL game, sent Sayers a telegram: "Congratulations on the greatest one-man performance I've ever witnessed on a football field."

No one in Wrigley Field would argue with that, least of all Sayers' teammates, who gave him the game ball for the second time that season, the first time any Bear had ever gotten two in one year. Some rookie!

Sayers ended the season with 22 touchdowns, a record that still stands, and he won the scoring title from Jimmy Brown, setting a record for rookies with 132 points. And, of course, he was the Rookie of the Year.

He went on setting records. In 1968, he piled up 2440 yards in total offense, leading the league with 1231 yards rushing and adding to this 447 yards in pass receptions, 718 in kickoff returns and 44 in punt returns. And after a crushing knee injury in 1968, he came back in 1969 to win the rushing title again with 1032 yards.

But, sadly, he injured his knee again in 1970 and in 1971 tried to play but couldn't. Now Gale Sayers is looking forward to running again in 1972.

Sayers loves playing football. Once, asked how he did a certain fake in a run, he said: "I have no idea what I do. I hear people talk about dead leg, shake, change of pace and all that, but I do things without thinking about them."

Fans who watched Sayers' matchless moves on a football field couldn't be quite sure what they saw either. What they saw was a magic that comes out of Gale Sayers. All they can be sure of is that they'd like to see it again. Especially that incredible year when Gale Sayers showed them what a great word "rookie" can be.

Rick Barry

Richard Francis Denny Barry III, the New York Nets 6'5" high-scoring forward, has played in the ABA since 1968, when he joined the Oakland Warriors. In that year, he won the ABA scoring championship, with 1190 points and a 34 point average.

Once, in the course of his extensive wanderings about the professional basketball world, Barry was part of the NBA. That was right after college in 1967-1968 when he played with the San Francisco Warriors. In that year, he won the NBA scoring title, with 2775 points and a 35.6 average.

Rick Barry is, consequently, the only man around who's led both leagues in scoring. And at the University of Miami, where he was an All-American, he topped all scorers in the NCAA with a 37.4 average.

The major and obvious conclusion to be drawn from all this is that Barry has a certain skill in putting a basketball through a hoop. In fact, he may well be the most potent scoring forward in the history of the game.

No less of a judge of basketball talent than Bill Sharman thinks so. Sharman, now coaching the Los Angeles Lakers, was Barry's coach when he was with the Warriors. "This far in his career," says Sharman, "I would have to rank Rick as the greatest and most productive forward ever to play the game. I think he's better than Elgin Baylor, Paul Arizin and Dolph Shayes, and they were all tremendous."

Barry's been accused of being just a "gunner," a player who's solely concerned with his scoring average. This is not true in Sharman's estimation. "Not only is Rick a great shooter," Sharman says, "he's also one of the game's finest passers. He hits the open man when he's double-teamed, which is often, and runs the pick and roll, setting up the other guys for easy layups, better than any player I've ever seen."

When he's hot Barry is totally dazzling. He shoots jumpers from outside the ABA's 25-foot circle for three points, inside it for two. He drives in for layups, hits on hooks and fade-aways. He's brilliant from the foul-line as well, and in 1970-71 he led the ABA in foul-shooting percentage with an .890 mark on 451 free throws.

One of his greatest assets is that he's incredibly "quick" for a big man, which makes defending him extremely difficult. He uses his quickness to beat a taller defender, and his height to go over a smaller one.

In the first game of the 1972 playoffs against the Kentucky Colonels, Barry scored 50 points on a dazzling variety of shots. The Colonel's coach, Joe Mullaney, said: "We have a real problem with him. He can do just about anything he wants to in a game, and our big problem is that we don't have anyone who can really handle him."

During the 1971-72 season, Barry had a number of nights when he couldn't be handled, and, as a result, the "lowly," lightly-regarded Nets came to within two games of winning the league championship. Barry's play throughout the year confirmed Sharman's judgment of him as not only a shooter but a team man. Early in December, one-third of the way through the season, the Nets were floundering in fifth place with an 11-16 record. Barry was hitting well, but the team was not playing well as a team. Barry was hopeful: "Maybe we'll put it together yet," he said, but it seemed a faint hope.

Gradually, however, as the season moved along, the Nets did begin to put it together, becoming a much more disciplined and cohesive unit. The passing and rebounding improved considerably. And Barry was the cornerstone on which the success of the team rested. He was the big gun, averaging better than 30 points a game, and now when he had an off-night, Billy Paultz, Bill Melchionni or

John Roche, the rookie from the University of South Carolina, took up the scoring slack.

But most frequently Barry's baskets led the way to a Net victory. Barry is an intense competitor, and often he came through with the winning baskets in the closing minutes of a close game. In a game against Memphis, for instance, which the Nets won 103-101, he coolly put in the last shot with two seconds remaining after the Nets held the ball for close to 30 seconds. He poured in 45 points against the Denver Rockets in the Nets inaugural game in their new home, the Nassau Coliseum. Against the Pittsburgh Condors he hit five out of seven three-pointers (to set a Nets' record) as the Nets won 133-123. Perhaps his most sensational shooting display of the season came in a game against the Rockets in Denver, when he hit three three-pointers in a row in 45 seconds.

The Nets ended the season in third place in the eastern division. They were heavy underdogs as they went into the playoffs against the Kentucky Colonels, led by Dan Issel and 7'2" Artis Gilmore, called "the Intimidator" because of all the shots he blocks. Kentucky had the best won-lost percentage any team ever achieved in the ABA and finished 24 games ahead of the Nets.

But the Nets outplayed them and won the series 4-2. Barry got the Nets off to an excellent start with his 50 points in the first game, hitting 18 of 28 from the floor. After the game, he said: "I don't think it's necessary for me to score 50 for us to win. What we need is contributions from everybody." That's what they got. Barry came down with the flu; he missed one game and played below his best in the final game. But the Nets won without him.

The Nets next took on the Virginia Squires, paced by forward Julius Erving. Again the Nets were underdogs and again they won, 4-3. Barry scored consistently in the series but the victory was clearly a team effort.

Against the Indiana Pacers, in the championship finals, the Nets came to the end of the road. But not without putting up a good fight. Barry was the hero when he tied the series 1-1 as the Nets won on his last-second jumper, 117-115. He made a rare mistake in the fifth game when he let a

Barry is one of the best marksmen in ABA.

pass go through his hands in the closing moments. The Nets missed an opportunity to try for the tying shot and lost 100-99.

A couple of days before the final game, Barry hurt his shoulder in practice. He took a shot of novacain before the game and scored 23 points. But his playing was below par and the Pacers won 108-105 to take the series and the championship.

In 18 playoff games, Barry scored 564 points for a 31.3 average to lead the Nets. His playoff average was very close to his season's average of 31.4, second best in the ABA.

"We surprised a lot of people this year," Barry said after the final game. That was true. But Barry surprised no one by playing as well as he did.

Lance Alworth

On a football field, Lance Alworth is something to see. When he was playing for Brookhaven High School in Brookhaven, Mississippi, an opposing high school coach said, "Alworth is the only high school back I've ever seen who can leap over the line and keep going without missing a step. He reminds me of that little deer in Walt Disney." The coach was thinking of Bambi, of course, and that name has stuck. Even Alworth's pro teammates on the San Diego Chargers called him that as they marveled at the wide receiver's fluid grace in making tumbling, diving "impossible" catches.

Alworth's playing style is, indeed, awe-inspiring, and many a fan has held his breath watching Alworth launch himself skyward in a crowd of defensive backs to grab the ball, expecting to see him crumple to the ground when he was hit.

But Alworth himself plays down the danger. "Some guys flinch," he says. "Maybe instead of flinching I leap. I feel I'm probably in better shape than people who have their feet on the ground. When I get hit, they're just going to push me forward or turn me end over. People who have their feet on the ground are going to get twisted."

Still, whether or not his daring style has been responsible, Alworth has nursed a variety of breaks, sprains and bruises over the years, from cracked ribs to broken wrists. Only the most serious of these, however, has kept him off the field. One of the smaller men in the game at 6', 180 pounds, Alworth has a fantastic determination to play, and play well. He says, "People keep writing that I have a history of injuries. Well, I've been hurt some, but the thing is I *play*. Except for my rookie year I've played nearly every game."

In his rookie year, 1962, when he joined San Diego after a brilliant college career at the University of Arkansas, Alworth was a victim of the rookie's worst nightmare: he hurt his leg in practice, not running for a pass, but attempting to place kick. He missed 10 of the Chargers 14 games. The injury, diagnosed as a pulled muscle in his thigh, cut down considerably on his speed and deception. And it didn't seem to heal. There were even some remarks to the effect that Alworth was afraid of playing pro ball. After the season, doctors discovered that the muscle was torn and Alworth had an operation to fix it.

He came back strong in 1963, pushing himself through a tough conditioning program in the off-season, to catch 61 passes and make the AFL all-star team. That was just the beginning: by the end of the 1969 season Lance Alworth had established himself as a true super-star, a player who had turned the record books inside out, one of the greatest pass-catchers in all football history.

From 1963 through 1969, Alworth gained more than 1000 yards each season on pass receptions, a pro record. And in December 1969, he set the record that will undoubtedly stand for quite a number of years to come, catching at least one pass in 96 consecutive games, to break the mark of 95 set 24 years before by Don Hutson. The game was stopped and Hutson himself walked out on the field to congratulate Alworth. "It's a pleasure to lose it to a fellow like Lance," Hutson said. "The man is terrific." Fittingly enough, the pass Alworth caught to break Hutson's mark was for a touchdown.

At that point it seemed as if Lance Alworth was sitting on top of the world. Not yet 30, he had a lot of good years left, a lot more time to set more records. His life so far seemed to mark him as a "golden boy" who would climb ever higher. He grew up in a small town in Mississippi, the son of an oil executive, was a standout in every sport he played (he won 15 letters in high school and was offered $25,000 to sign with the Yankees as a shortstop). Athletic endowment ran in the family; his father ran track, several uncles played college football. It was football that Alworth loved best, and he went on to the University of Arkansas to star in that sport. He led Arkansas to three Southwest Conference championships as a running back, was an All-America halfback, led the country in punt returns as a junior.

When he chose San Diego of the AFL over San Francisco Alworth knew he was going to "the new league," regarded by many fans as being far below the level of the NFL. Alworth helped change that image with his superlative play.

Then came 1970. Suddenly things went bad for Alworth off the field. His marriage to his childhood sweetheart failed. Business deals which had promised to make him a millionaire went sour. His performance on the field reflected these problems and at the end of the season, he was traded to the Dallas Cowboys.

Alworth was unhappy at first, but when, as he said, he "thought about Dallas and looked at their record," he decided that his first reaction, to quit the game, was a hasty one, and he went to Dallas determined to come back strong.

Right at the start, it seemed as if the miseries of 1970 would continue on into '71 for Alworth. In an early exhibition game against Cleveland, he went up high for a pass and was caught like a walnut by two crunching defensive backs. Result: five cracked ribs, the loss of both big toenails when the defensive back crushed his feet. Taped up,

visiting the doctor regularly, Alworth continued to work out. As he has said, he *plays*.

Alworth worked right into the Dallas offense. Speedster Bob Hayes took the secondary long, Alworth looped out for short gainers 10 and 20 yards from scrimmage. In a vital game against the Los Angeles Rams, with both teams fighting to get into the Super Bowl, Alworth scored his first touchdown as a Cowboy, cutting across the field in beautifully controlled motion to take a 21-yard pass from Dallas quarterback Roger Staubach after Hayes pulled the secondary away from the spot.

Victory in that game pushed the Cowboys toward the Super Bowl, and when they squared off against the Miami Dolphins, Alworth was ready. Gone were the worries of the previous season. He'd proved that he still had it, catching 34 passes for 487 yards and two touchdowns for Dallas. Now he was playing in the championship game.

Sizing up the Cowboys before the game, Baltimore coach Don McCafferty spoke of Alworth's "great moves." Alworth showed 81,000 fans in New Orleans and millions of others watching on television just what McCafferty was talking about.

The Cowboys were ahead 3-0 on a first period field goal by Mike Clark when Roger Staubach started Dallas moving at the close of the second quarter. On third and nine, he hit Alworth with a 21-yard pass to the Dolphins 33. Alworth sneaked between Miami defenders Doug Swift and Dick Anderson on a beautifully-executed pattern.

Four plays later, with the Cowboys on the Dolphins seven yard line and just 75 seconds left in the half, Alworth, lining up as the wide receiver, floated down into the left corner. He was guarded by Curtis Johnson. Staubach threw a perfectly-timed pass, and Alworth timed his pattern just as perfectly. He flashed in front of Johnson, who had no chance to play the ball, grabbed the chest-high pass and stepped into the end zone.

That was the winning score. Miami came back to score a field goal before the half ended, but the second half was all Dallas, the final score 24-3. Earlier in the season, after he caught his first touchdown pass for Dallas, Alworth said, "Now I feel like a Cowboy." After the Super Bowl, he could feel like a champion, too.

Willis Reed

At 7:34, exactly one minute before the official starting time of the game, Willis Reed came out of the dressing room and on to the floor of Madison Square Garden. The overflow crowd rose to its feet and cheered, and the sound was loud and exultant. *He's going to play,* was the thought that prompted the noise. Fans, Knicks and Los Angeles Lakers watched closely as Reed took some practice shots. Moving purposefully but without a limp, he sank the first shot and people in the stands began to smile.

Earlier, around 6:30, Reed had come out to practice a bit, but no one knew if he'd actually be playing or not. Then he went back into the dressing room while the rest of the Knicks continued to warm up. Moments before he came out for the second time, he took an injection in his right thigh. The needle was six inches long. It contained cortisone and carbocaine, a pain-killer, and if they worked well, these drugs would erase the pain of the two torn muscles in Reed's leg.

The national anthem sounded, the teams lined up. It was the final game in the playoffs for the championship of the NBA. Each team had won three games. New York had gone 24 years without a title. The Lakers had been in the finals seven times. They had yet to win. But in the sixth game, played in Los Angeles, the Lakers had overwhelmed New York 135-113. Reed had not played, and without Reed to hold him down, Wilt Chamberlain dominated the game, hitting 45 points. If Reed could not perform well this evening, the Lakers felt that the 1970 championship would be theirs. The Knicks felt the same way, and they watched anxiously as Reed set himself to jump against Chamberlain....

Willis Reed came to the Knicks as a second round draft choice in 1964. Born in 1942, he grew up in Bernice, Louisiana, and went to Grambling College. An All-American, 6'10" and 240 pounds, Reed played center his first year in the NBA, averaged 19.5 points and was Rookie of the Year. Then the Knicks acquired Walt Bellamy, bigger than Reed. Switched to forward, Reed played that position for three years, never really comfortable although he was an All-Star forward, until the Knicks traded for Dave DeBusschere in 1968 and Reed happily moved back to center.

The Knick team facing the Lakers in the play-offs, coached by Red Holzman, had come together in fantastic style during the 1969-1970 season. Walt Frazier and Dick Barnett at guards, Bill Bradley and DeBusschere at forwards, Reed at center— they worked beautifully together. They were all good shooters. They played tight defense, passed off to each other, set up plays to spring an open man. DeBusschere was excellent under the boards. Reed was big enough and strong enough to handle any center in the league, including the massive Chamberlain. He shot extremely well and was a marvelous rebounder. On offense and defense, he was the kingpin of the team.

At the start of the season, the Knicks won 23 of 25 games, including 18 straight, then an NBA record, and advanced through the playoff rounds by beating the Baltimore Bullets and the Milwaukee Bucks.

Reed had a marvelous year of his own—1126 rebounds, 1755 points, a 21.7 scoring average, the highest on the Knicks. Before the playoffs, he was named the league's Most Valuable Player.

He had a lot of good nights, some really phenomenal ones. On a trip west at the beginning of November, he scored 35 against Kareem

Reed jumps high shooting against 76ers.

Reed, said: "He was charged up. Super quick. We were all a step behind him."

Against the Lakers and Wilt Chamberlain, himself recovering from knee surgery, Reed was solid. Then, in the fifth game in L.A. with the teams tied 2-2 in games, Reed tore his thigh muscles and had to sit down. The Knicks scrambled out of that hole, coming from 16 points behind to win. But Reed returned to New York for treatment right after the game, and Chamberlain scored 45 in the sixth game to even the series.

Now Reed was out on the floor again. On the Knicks' first play, Reed took a jump shot from the top of the key and scored. The crowd roared. Walt Frazier said to himself: "He ain't hurt."

At the other end of the court, Wilt Chamberlain stationed himself to the left of the lane. His spot. He got the ball and tried to move left and in. Reed stayed with him, stopped him, despite the bad leg. Chamberlain threw the ball out. After that, he didn't try to go left anymore. He took all his shots from the right, tried nine, made two and ended the night with just 13 points.

Moving down to the Knicks' end, Reed sank another basket. That was all the scoring he was to do for the evening. It was enough. His clamp on Chamberlain and his psychological effect on the Knicks and the Lakers decided the game. The Knicks ran, stole the ball, scored. The Lakers seemed to stand around a lot, watching the action. When Reed left with 3:05 to go in the first half, New York led 61-37. Reed came back in for a few minutes in the third quarter, then limped to the bench to sit out the rest of the game. Walt Frazier took up the scoring slack with 36 points. The final score was 113-99 and the Knicks were truly Number One.

"When Willis Reed stepped on the court," Bill Bradley said later, "it gave us a 10-foot lift." Dick Barnett took the opposing view: "It was a psych on the Lakers," he said.

Reed's appearance was one of the most dramatic in sports—and one of the most courageous. He was in pain the whole game, unable to push off with his right leg. Even after he got a second shot between halves, the pain returned. "It was rough," he said later. "The leg started to hurt from the opening jump. But I had to be there."

Abdul-Jabbar, 34 against the Phoenix Suns, 26 against San Diego and 35 against Wilt Chamberlain in Los Angeles. In the fifth game of the playoffs in Baltimore, Reed was nothing short of sensational. Playing against Wes Unseld, an excellent rebounder, Reed dropped in 36 points and grabbed 36 rebounds (a Knick record). He was all over the court, seemed to know exactly where the ball was going to come off of the backboard and boxed Unseld out time after time. Ray Scott, who replaced Unseld and tried to contain

Bobby Orr

Bobby Orr keeps inventing new and better ways to play hockey. They're not very practical, of course, because he's the only one who can make them work. But they are interesting to watch.

In the 1972 Stanley Cup playoffs against the New York Rangers, for example, Orr introduced a fairly dazzling new move in the sixth and final game. He got the puck at the blue line while the Rangers were one man short. Bruce MacGregor, a New York penalty killer; skated toward him and poked his stick at the puck, hoping to take it away. If he did, he'd have a breakaway shot at the Boston goal.

But trying to take the puck away from Orr is like trying to rob Fort Knox. Theoretically, it can be done. But it doesn't happen too often. Orr pulled the puck back, pirouetted on his left skate in a 180 degree circle, moved in on the Ranger goal and from 35 feet out snapped off a wrist shot that sailed past Ranger goalie Ed Giacomin's left leg to make the score 1-0.

A play like that does more than put a goal on the scoreboard. It also makes an opposing team feel like it left hockey school too soon. Orr himself may have been a little astounded by his play on MacGregor. After the game, he said: "I don't know if that was a new move, but I do know I almost lost the puck."

Leading Boston to its second Stanley Cup in four years, Orr ended up with four goals and four assists, more than any other player, dominated on defense as well as offense, and, not surprisingly, was awarded the Conn Smythe Trophy as the playoff's Most Valuable Player.

He could put this on the shelf next to his other awards in 1972: the James Norris Memorial Trophy as the best defenseman (he's the first player ever to win it five years straight), and the Hart Memorial Trophy as the league's Most Valuable Player, which he won for the third straight time, the first player ever to do that.

Robert Gordon Orr, the blond, 24-year-old baby-faced defenseman for the Boston Bruins is, beyond argument, the most gifted hockey player in the history of the game. And after just six seasons in the NHL, he is already being spoken of as the greatest all-around player hockey has ever known.

And with good reason. Listing his specific talents doesn't begin to tell the story. He is a brilliant skater who has, as Boston defenseman Teddy Green says, "18 speeds of fast." His shot is fast and "heavy"—hard to handle. His slap shot has been clocked at 110 miles per hour, second only to Bobby Hull's, and Orr gets his away quicker. He has an uncanny hockey sense which tells him, before other men know, where the puck is going, how a play will unfold. With these skills, Orr produces hockey that is consistently spectacular, game after game coming up with moves that make the other players gasp with amazement. As the Bruins' general manager, Milt Schmidt, says, "You watch him every game and you say, 'there's the best play he's every made.' Then you look again and he's doing something even better."

Orr was born in Parry Sound, Ontario, in 1948. He was on skates three years later, had a hockey stick in his hands when he was four and at five was playing in an organized league in Parry Sound. His father was an exceptional player who might have made it to the NHL if World War II hadn't come along. When he was 12, Bobby was spotted by a Boston scout, and the Bruins kept close tabs on him thereafter, arranging for him to play in a higher league and finally signing him in 1966.

When Bobby Orr joined the Bruins, the team had not won the Stanley Cup since 1941, had not even made the playoffs in seven years and had finished last in the standings in five of the past six years. Boston's management believed so strongly in Orr's capacity to turn the team around that they gave him a two year contract for $75,000, an astounding sum in hockey at that time for a rookie—and more money than any Boston player was making.

Orr was of course worth every penny. Not only was he capable of doing astonishing things with stick and skates, he was totally unafraid physically. Not very big at 5'11" and 185 pounds, he is stronger than he looks. At the beginning, he had any number of fights to prove he couldn't be pushed around. Beyond that, he skated at top speed into precarious and dangerous situations and seemed never to worry about hurting himself.

In his rookie year he had 41 points, including 13 goals, and was named Rookie of the Year. And the next season, 1967-68, despite injuries that kept him out of 28 games—in the course of a year, he had three knee operations, a broken collarbone, a shoulder separation and several broken noses—he won the Norris Trophy, made the first All-Star team and led the Bruins into the playoffs.

That was worth a new three-year contract, first said to be for $400,000, later for $200,000. Either way, it was a great deal of money for a player starting his third season (and it led to a whole new salary scale in the NHL).

Orr only received that kind of money because he so obviously could command it. Fans loved to watch him play, and he made the Bruins a superior force almost singlehandedly—although even an Orr has to have some help, and it was when Boston got Phil Esposito, Ken Hodge and Fred Stanfield from Chicago that they began to play winning hockey.

Leading the way was the fabulous Orr. In 1968-69 he emerged as the game's most offensive defenseman. In that season, Boston finished second and Orr scored 64 points. He had 23 goals, a record for a defenseman, including the "hat trick"—three in one game—to go with his 41 assists and he won the Norris Trophy for the first time.

In his next season, 1969-70, Orr's hockey stick was a cannon that blew apart all previous scoring records for defensemen. Just before mid-season,

he was leading the league in scoring with 56 points on 11 goals and 45 assists. He finished out the year with 120 points, tops in the league, twice as many as a defenseman ever scored before, and he set an NHL record for assists with 87 and for goals by a defenseman with 33. At the same time, amazingly, Orr continued as the game's most brilliant defenseman, again winner of the Norris Trophy.

Orr maintained the superlative level of his play in the Stanley Cup playoffs. Against the Rangers in the first round, he scored seven goals, a record for a defenseman, and simply carried the Bruins to victory.

In the sixth and final game, Orr started off by tying the score on a "nobody but Orr could do it" goal, in which he deflected a shot by Wayne Cashman past Giacomin, curling the puck in the curved part of his stick to steer it. With the score 2-1, Orr got a goal on a slap shot from the right boards that Giacomin never saw until it was past him, and Boston added a goal to make the final score 4-1. Against Chicago and St. Louis in the next two rounds, Orr was equally devastating, and the Bruins won against both teams in four straight to become Stanley Cup champions.

Orr is now firmly established as a new kind of defenseman, one who is more of an offensive threat than all but a few offensive players in the league. In both 1971 and 1972, he finished second in scoring to Phil Esposito.

The acknowledged leader of the Bruins, Orr has proven that he's all for the team, and his teammates themselves are in awe of what he does in the rink. On top of that, he is universally regarded as the world's nicest guy. As for how he does what he does, Orr himself says: "I can't explain it. They all ask me, 'What were you thinking when you started up ice?' and things like that. Hockey is not that type of game. Things happen too fast. We don't have any real planned plays, like in football. I skate up ice and look. I don't know what I'm going to do until it's done. You just adjust to the situation. If the defense is split too wide I'll try to go through. If the defense is closed, I pass the puck. But I never know what's going to happen until I get there."

Neither do the players opposing him—except that it won't be good for them.

Bob Griese

Second play of the game, second and five on Miami's 25. Bob Griese called signals, took the ball. Faking a handoff, he looked for the man he'd sent down field, Miami's fast, tricky wide receiver, Paul Warfield. Colt cornerback Rex Kern bumped Warfield to delay him—but the delay was only momentary. Warfield took off like the rabbit he is. Griese's beautifully arched spiral dropped into Warfield's waiting arms—and Kern couldn't have caught him on a motorcycle. Miami, 7-0.

The Baltimore Colts never did recover from that devastating bomb, artfully called by Griese. An intercepted Unitas pass in the third quarter, another pass from Griese to Warfield in the fourth, and the final score was 21-0, the first time the Colts had been shut out in 96 games. Miami had won the American Conference title and would face the Dallas Cowboys in the 1972 Super Bowl.

It was a great end to the 1972 season for quarterback Bob Griese and the Miami Dolphins. Directing the Dolphins to the conference title, Griese had established himself as a cool, quick-thinking field general, a strong, accurate passer with a quick release second only to Joe Namath's, and a scrambler who could get yards on the ground when they were needed. It was largely due to his performance throughout the year that the young, unheralded Dolphins were now in reach of football's biggest prize.

Just 26 years old, the blond, blue-eyed Griese already has five years of pro experience behind him. He came to the Dolphins as their first draft choice in 1967 after an outstanding career as a quarterback at Purdue. In his junior year, he led the Big Ten in passing. In a game against Notre Dame, Griese hit 19 of 22 as the Boilermakers won 25-21. Notre Dame's coach, Ara Parseghian, said after the game that this was "the greatest performance I have ever seen from the sideline." Purdue went to the Rose Bowl in Griese's senior year and beat USC 14-13.

Griese got a chance to play at Miami sooner than a rookie quarterback normally would because Miami's first string quarterback broke his leg in the first game of the season. For three years, however, until ex-Baltimore coach Don Shula took over, Miami had a mediocre record. Under Shula, Griese became much less of a throwing quarterback and much more of a quarterback directing a running attack. Griese was well suited for this role.

"In a game," Griese says, "I think of myself as looking down on a situation from above, like a chess player moving chesspieces. I can see moves coming and I'm ready to make them." In the Baltimore game, for example, Griese called for the second-and-five pass to Warfield because he saw things that made him believe Baltimore would be playing Warfield one on one, instead of in a zone or with the double coverage he usually gets.

His Miami teammates have a high regard for Griese's knowledge of the game and for his football intelligence, and so do opposition players. Buffalo safety Pete Richardson, for instance, says: "He always seems to know which way I'm going. Like I'll take two steps to the right when he's counting and it's like he's looking into my head and he knows I have to come back these two steps before the ball is snapped."

Griese is just as happy not throwing as many passes, and during the 1971 season, in fact, his best games were those in which he threw 10 passes instead of the 45 he used to throw. "He likes being able to take advantage of the system," says Shula, "and he enjoys calling the right play."

And he makes the system work, as he did in the game preceding the Baltimore game when Miami

Griese led young Miami team into the Super Bowl in big surprise of 1971 season.

played the Kansas City Chiefs. This turned into the longest game on record, an 82-minute affair that ran five quarters plus before it was finally settled when Garo Yepremian kicked a 37-yard field goal to make the score 27-24.

Kansas City had stopped Miami's running game for the most part, and Griese took to the air, completing 20 passes for 263 yards. But Griese set up the winning field goal by calling the perfect play, and it was not a pass. It was a "roll right, trap left" in which Kiick and Griese move to the left and Csonka follows for a step, then cuts back to the right. Csonka went from Miami's 35 to the Kansas 36 and the field goal followed. Kansas City obviously did not expect the play. "We hadn't used it yet," Griese said after the game, "and it seemed like the right time for it."

Griese has put in long hours studying the complications of opposing defenses, looking over and over again at films showing how linebackers and cornerbacks and safety men react.

He is expert on recognizing blitzes and calling audibles to thwart them. "It's a funny thing," he says, "but sometimes you can look in a defenseman's eyes and you can *tell* they're blitzing." More often, Griese recognizes a blitz because someone is doing something he didn't do before or not doing something he did do. To Griese, there is "no great mystery to quarterbacking. You move guys around in different formations, looking for the weak spot."

That of course is what Griese tried to do when Miami met the Dallas Cowboys in the Super Bowl. But the game was all Dallas, with Miami managing to get just one field goal in a 24-3 defeat. The Miami attack never developed any juice, either on the ground or in the air, and Dallas got the jump on every move Miami tried to make. For example, Chuck Howley intercepted a pass intended for Jim Kiick and returned it 41 yards to set up a touchdown. Griese said of that play: "Howley had fallen down on that play trying to cut down the flanker. I saw him fall and went to Kiick, but it was unbelievable how fast Howley got up and recovered. You don't expect that much speed."

Disappointed as he was over the Super Bowl result, Griese had one consolation. It came five months later when he was honored in New York as the outstanding player on the losing team, while tackle Bob Lilly was honored from the winners. It's a pretty good bet that Bob Griese is devoting himself right now to the subject of how to change sides the next time around.

Hank Aaron

Sometime during the next two seasons, in 1973 or 1974, Hank Aaron will almost surely break the most famous, sought-after and "unattainable" record in baseball, one that has been in the books— a towering but faraway peak—for more than 35 years. He will step to the plate, take his smooth, wrist-snapping swing and send a ball sailing into the stands for the 715th home run of his career.

He will then have hit one more home run than the great Babe Ruth, and he will be engulfed in a wave of publicity that will make him as famous as any ballplayer can be. When this happens, fans will discover that the quiet, conservative right fielder on the Atlanta Braves is probably the greatest ballplayer of his era—and, in some ways, of all time.

Hank Aaron has never played with the flamboyance of Willie Mays, has never captured the public imagination like Mickey Mantle. All during his career, particularly up until the last three or four years, Aaron's exploits on the ball field have never received quite the attention they have deserved. For this reason, when all-time greats are mentioned, Aaron is often overlooked.

Yet "Hammering Hank" is the holder of an astounding collection of records. His home run total (currently more than 640) is only the beginning of the story. In the other categories usually considered most important in rating a hitter, Aaron ranks equally high. As of the end of the 1971 season, he had these totals:
• Hits: 3272, sixth on the all-time list behind Ty Cobb, Stan Musial, Tris Speaker, Honus Wagner and Eddie Collins. (He will move up to fifth during the 1972 season.) Only ten men in all baseball history have ever had more than 3000 hits.
• Total Bases: 5941, second behind Musial. (He

could move up to first during the 1972 season.)
• Extra Base Hits: 1296, third behind Musial and Babe Ruth. (He could move up to first during the 1972 season.)
• Runs Batted In: 1960, third behind Ruth and Lou Gehrig. (He will move up to second during the 1972 season.)
• Slugging Percentage: .569, eighth on the all-time list. Ruth is first with .692.

Aaron is more than a great hitter. He is the complete ball player. As Mickey Mantle said, "Henry Aaron is the best ballplayer of my era. He is to baseball of the last 15 years what Joe DiMaggio was before him." An excellent fielder, Aaron has a good, strong arm and solid speed and skill on the basepaths. "Henry could steal 50 bases a year, if he wanted to," Roger Maris has said. "In some ways it's unfortunate his hitting is so outstanding. It tends to overshadow his other talents." Aaron has in fact stolen 20 or more bases six times in his career, and reached 31 in 1963.

Durability and consistency have been the hallmarks of Aaron's career. He's hit more than 40 home runs seven times, a National League record. His lifetime batting average at the end of the 1971 season was .313, topped among active players only by Roberto Clemente. His highest mark was .355 in 1955 when he won the batting title, his lowest .279 in 1966. Now in his 19th season, Hank has played less than 150 games only three times and has gone to bat more than 10,000 times.

Physically, he's a young 38, in excellent condition, lean and compact, despite an arthritic neck and shoulder that act up in cold weather. His knee did bother him in 1971 and he had it drained several times. But over the winter, he lifted weights with it and it has been fine so far in 1972.

Just 20 when he came up to the Braves in 1954, Aaron remarkably had only two years of organized baseball behind him. He was born and grew up in Mobile, Alabama. Since he went to a high school that had no baseball team, he played softball and football. But he wanted to be a professional ball-player and felt that baseball was his best bet, so he began playing baseball with a semi-professional team. At 18, he joined the Indianapolis Clowns in the Negro American League, got 10 hits in his first 11 times at bat and was hitting more than .400 after 15 games. He quickly attracted the attention of Braves' and Giants' scouts. The Braves grabbed him first, and after two seasons in the minors, playing shortstop and second, he was called up to Milwaukee in 1954 and switched to the outfield.

Aaron does not have the physique of a slugger—he's 6', 180 pounds. He began to splinter the fences when he switched to a lighter bat, one he could whip around at the last second to take advantage of his incredible wrists and eye. With this bat he went from a .280 average and 13 home runs in 1954 to a .314 average, 27 home runs and 106 runs batted in the next year. Henry had arrived!

His third year in the majors, Aaron won the batting championship, hitting .328. In 1957, he hit .322, had 132 runs batted in, 44 home runs and was named the league's Most Valuable Player. The Braves won the pennant both years. Aaron broke up a 2-2 ball game with a homer in the eleventh inning to clinch the victory for Milwaukee in 1957, then hit .393 for the Series as the Braves beat the Yankees.

Since then, Aaron has led the league in homers three times, in runs batted in twice, but Milwaukee has not won a pennant, which may be one reason why Aaron has not received the attention he's deserved.

Another reason is, very definitely, his personality and philosophy. Quiet and self-contained, Aaron has gone about doing his job in the most efficient and least demonstrative way. When he first came up to the majors, he was young, shy and wary. He deliberately cultivated the reputation of being a "sleepyhead" who was, perhaps, a little "slow."

Actually highly intelligent, Aaron missed nothing. He can, within reason, name the exact kind of pitch he has hit for homer after homer. And he can tell you why the pitcher threw what he threw. For example, talking about homer number 600, which he hit at the beginning of the 1971 season against the Giants' Gaylord Perry, he said later: "I guessed fastball and got it. Perry tried to jam me, but missed by about two inches and I got a clean shot at it. I knew it was gone the minute I hit it."

In addition to his early "sleepyhead" disguise, Aaron has always operated on the philosophy that wasted effort is silly. Running bases, he goes as fast as he thinks he has to. "I'm watching the fielder," he says, "and I can accelerate—I have the speed to shift gears." Similarly, if he knows a ball is going foul, he won't chase it just to look good, as many outfielders do. "That's false hustle," he says.

What Aaron's interested in is the reality of the game, not the show. He has always loved playing baseball, and he is regarded as one of the most knowledgeable players in the game. Clete Boyer has said that Aaron "knows more baseball than any man I have ever met." A keen student of his own hitting, he knows exactly what he's doing at bat. "Moving the legs or opening and closing your stance is not as important as the upper part of the body," Aaron says. "It's the controlling of the bat that is important and being able to snap your wrists at the last instant that allows you to do something with a pitch you might have already been fooled on." Aaron's ability to snap his wrists with great speed is unparalleled. In his early years, he hit to all fields; now he primarily pulls to left, and this has been a big factor in his continued home run production.

Having hit an amazing 47 home runs at the age of 37 in 1971, Aaron almost seems to be improving with age. Pitcher Curt Simmons probably reflected the general feeling about Aaron's hitting when he said: "Throwing a fastball past Aaron is like trying to sneak the sun past a rooster." Maybe Casey Stengel, the old, amazin' master, had the solution for pitching to "Hammering Henry" Aaron: "You bounce it to the plate and walk him," Stengel said. "Then he steals second and you have an open base to operate with."

Dick Butkus

All men are created equal, but on a football field some men are more equal than others. Richard Marvin Butkus, the middle linebacker of the Chicago Bears is probably equal, on a good day—and he rarely has bad ones—to three normal defensive players. Butkus has been described as the toughest, angriest man playing the game. Whether or not he merits those labels, very few men in the NFL will argue with the conclusion that he's the best middle linebacker around today, probably the best ever.

Vince Lombardi, the great Green Bay Packers coach, thought so. When Butkus played against the Packers for the first time, Lombardi told his men: "Let's smear this kid's face." Butkus turned in his normal rampaging performance, roaming all over the field to shatter the Packer offense, and after the game Lombardi said, "He's the best who ever played the position."

Lombardi was not alone in his judgement. In a poll taken in 1970 by *Pro Football Weekly* a majority of the coaches polled named him as the man they would most like to have on their teams.

What makes Butkus so great? He's not that big, really, compared to some of the "monster men" now in the game. He's 6'3" and weighs 245. Still, one sports writer noted as he watched Butkus march onto the field, "He looks bigger than anyone else on the field...he has the biggest shoulders on earth...the entire alphabet could be printed on his uniform and there'd be room left over."

Besides his imposing appearance, Butkus has other qualifications for his job. A middle linebacker has to be strong, since he's constantly tossing around offensive linemen in his battle to get to the ball-carrier. He has to be fast, so that he can move to either side to stop end runs and drop back to cover pass receivers coming out of the backfield. He must also be smart enough to figure out, in split seconds, what awful surprises will be hatched by a complicated, deceptive offense.

Butkus excels in all these departments. He's very strong and very fast. As Bart Starr has said, "He covers so much ground—you can complete a pass downfield and, son of a gun, he makes the tackle." And his strength and quickness are backed up by a highly developed football intelligence. Butkus calls defensive signals for the Bears and is outstanding in his ability to sniff out what the offense is going to do.

"I can see it all happen," he says. "At the key moment—the instant of the snap—I somehow know, most of the time, just how the flow pattern will develop. I stare—I don't know—right *through* the center and the quarterback, right through their eyes. I watch for the keys, and they are very tiny keys, believe me. Tiny little twitches of their shoulders and their heads and their feet and their eyes. There's just this split second, before it all starts to move, when you put those keys together and you know—you just know—how it's going."

Because, most of the time, he knows how it's going, Butkus is murder on the blitz, that defensive maneuver in which a linebacker stampedes through the line to run over the quarterback.

What fuels these talents is Butkus' fierce desire. As Butkus himself says, "Every time I play a game

I want to play it as if it's my last one. You could get hurt and that would be it for keeps. I don't want my last game to be a lousy performance."

At the most elemental level, Dick Butkus simply loves to play football. He went to Chicago Vocational High School, even though it was farther away from his home than other schools, because its football coach was considered to be the best in Chicago. He played both offense and defense, was a high school All-America fullback and made 70 per cent of his team's tackles.

By the time he was ready for college, Butkus had offers from the best football schools in the country. He picked the University of Illinois because it was close to home and because he thought football in the Big Ten would be challenging. Butkus was tougher than the competition. In his junior year (1963), Illinois had a powerhouse team, winning the Big Ten Championship, then beating Washington in the Rose Bowl, 17-7. Butkus starred in game after game. He was all over the field, crashing through opposing linemen like an angry tank, intercepting passes, making dozens of tackles (23 against Ohio State, for example). He was a unanimous All-American choice that year and in his senior year was voted College Lineman of the Year. In 1969 he was picked for the All-Time All-America college team.

In his first year with the Bears, Butkus adjusted quickly to the pro game. All around the league, coaches and players pointed to Butkus as a very special football machine. He probably would have been named Rookie of the Year, but another rookie on the Bears, Gale Sayers, scored 22 touchdowns to win that honor.

The special machine has grown more finely tuned with the years, and its speciality is still an all-out physical commitment that sometimes makes Butkus seem like a force of nature, a cleated cyclone, swooping, veering, hurling his body in great arcs of destruction, laying waste opposing players.

As one Bear teammate says: "Butkus is simply the best. He's superman. He's the greatest thing since popcorn." ∎

Butkus calls defensive signals for Bears, is brilliant at guessing what offense will do.

Oscar Robertson

After Oscar Robertson and the Cincinnati Royals had played in Boston against the Celtics in November, 1960, Bill Sharman, then a guard on the Boston team, now the coach of the Los Angeles Lakers, gave his opinion of Robertson: "He has three or four fakes, all in the same move," Sharman said. "He is a big man with the moves of a really tremendous little man and he is always ready to whip off a pass that will lead to a basket if a teammate gets free."

The game against Boston was only Robertson's ninth game in the NBA. But Sharman's estimate of him stands up pretty well today as Robertson, now 31 years old, begins his thirteenth NBA season in the fall of 1972. And Robertson's statistics in that game stand up equally well. He scored 25 points while getting seven assists and six rebounds, leading the Royals, who finished in last place in the eastern division, to a victory over the NBA champion Lakers.

Robertson finished that first year with over 2000 points, was third in scoring in the league with a 30.5 average and first in assists, with 690, an average of better than nine assists per game.

There are a couple of conclusions to be drawn from all this. One is that Robertson, from the start of his career, had his brilliant talents totally under control. No rookie "learning season" for him. He simply put on a Royals' uniform, walked out on the court and became Oscar Robertson, super-star. Of course the achievements that would gain him general recognition as such had to pile up over the years. But from the first "three or four fakes in one move," it was or should have been obvious that Robertson was on a very special line to greatness.

Control is behind the second conclusion as well. Over the years he's been in the NBA, Robertson has been incredibly consistent. Playing for the Royals from 1960 through 1970 (when he was traded to the Milwaukee Bucks), Robertson averaged 29.3 points a game and had just two years when his season's scoring average wandered more than two points above or below 30. Similarly, the number of assists he's totaled each year remain remarkably consistent also. In his 10 years as a Royal, he's averaged 10 assists per game.

And his totals are equally remarkable. At the end of the 1970-71 season, Robertson had scored 23,578 points. This put him second to Wilt Chamberlain on the all-time scoring list. In assists, he was at the top of the all-time list, his total of 8399 giving him a lead of more than a thousand over the second man, Bob Cousy of the Celtics, and more than three thousand over the Lakers' Jerry West.

Robertson accomplished these scoring feats despite being double-teamed very often, and despite being roughed-up by the opposition, which knew very well he was the man who made the Royals go. As Ed Juker, the Royals' coach during most of the period Oscar played there, has said: "Oscar continues to amaze me, no matter how many times I see him play. The physical beating he takes is sometimes unbelievably punishing."

Robertson changed the style of his game when he was traded from Cincinnati to the Milwaukee Bucks. In his first season with Milwaukee, 1970-71, he dipped ten points below his lifetime scoring average of 29.3 with an average of just 19.4 points per game. The change came because Robertson shifted his style to fit in with the Bucks' strategy. Milwaukee's attack is of course built around Kareem Abdul-Jabbar, and so Robertson shot a lot less. Highly intelligent, Robertson is an acute student of the game. "When you start plays," he said, "you rarely take a shot. You get your shots when you finish them." Starting plays that got the ball to Abdul-Jabbar, Robertson and the Bucks operated so successfully that Milwaukee won its first NBA title in 1971.

So much in control of his talents is Robertson that whenever Abdul-Jabbar wasn't operating at peak efficiency, and the Bucks needed points, Oscar was capable immediately of taking up the slack. In the 1971 title playoff against the Baltimore Bullets, for example, Kareem committed three quick fouls in the first period of the first game and sat down for the rest of the half. When he left, the Bucks were four points ahead. When he returned, they were eight points ahead. Robertson directed the team's attack beautifully, at the same time that he was scoring 15 points.

In functioning as more of a playmaker than a shooter with Milwaukee, Robertson also pressed a lot harder on defense. While he was at Cincinnati, he was not considered to be a really brilliant defensive player. But the Bucks' coach, Larry Costello, believes that Robertson's defensive contributions to Milwaukee have been enormously important.

Costello says: "Oscar has helped us as much on defense as on offense. He plays even better defense than Walt Frazier. He's stronger than Frazier, and nobody's going to take him inside and get six-foot shots. If anyone scores against Oscar, they're going to do it on 18-footers."

The Baltimore Bullets coach, Gene Shue, agrees: "Robertson should have been on the all-defensive team," Shue said after the 1971 season. "He got my vote. He may have played better defense than any other guard in the league."

Versatility such as this, exercised on the level of excellence that is habitual with Robertson, makes many observers feel that he is the best all-around player in the history of the game. Robertson began honing this excellence playing basketball at the "Y" in the Indianapolis neighborhood where he grew up. His older brothers were good basketball players, and they often didn't want to bother with "small fry" Oscar. That made him vow that he'd become better at the game than they were.

He practiced constantly and by the time he was a junior in high school, having grown to 6'5", he was the star of Crispus Atticus High School in Indianapolis. A Black high school had never won a state championship. Robertson led the school to state titles in his junior and senior years and in both years he was named to the high school All-American team.

At Cincinnati University, Robertson became equally outstanding. As a sophomore, he gained national recognition when he came into New York's Madison Square Garden and poured in 56 points against Seton Hall University to break the Garden scoring record. He ended up setting collegiate scoring records by averaging 33.9 points a game and scoring a total of 2973 points. These records stood until "Pistol Pete" Maravich broke them in 1969.

Robertson was pointing for a professional basketball career, but immediately after graduation he took time off to co-captain the championship United States Olympic basketball team (along with Jerry West).

When he joined the Royals in the fall of '60, he immediately became a big box office attraction. And equally important, he turned Cincinnati into a far stronger team. The Royals made it into the playoffs six of the 10 years Robertson was with them. But they never were able to win the title.

Joining the Bucks for the 1970-71 season, Robertson immediately made them a good prospect to take the NBA title. As the season progressed, it became obvious that Milwaukee with Robertson was a powerhouse club. The Bucks finished the season setting a record for shooting accuracy, becoming the first team in NBA history to hit better than 50 per cent of their shots over the course of a season. And in the final playoff, against the Baltimore Bullets, Milwaukee showed its power by taking the series in four straight games, the first time this had ever happened. In the fourth and clinching game, Robertson put on a patented Big O performance. He hit 11 of 15 shots from the field, made eight of nine free throws and was credited with nine assists.

Robertson had not been on a championship team since high school. In the locker room, as the Bucks celebrated their victory, Robertson raised a glass of champagne and said: "This is the first champagne I've ever had and it tastes mighty sweet."

Carl Yastrzemski

When Carl Yastrzemski was 18 months old, his father, Carl, Sr., gave him a tiny baseball bat. It became his favorite toy. When he was six, Carl batted against his father's pitching every night after supper in the backyard of the Yastrzemski home in Bridgehampton, Long Island, hitting tennis balls out over the lawn. On his grandfather's potato farm, he fungoed tiny potatoes out into the fields all day while his grandfather worked. Carl would go through the line-up of his two favorite teams, the New York Yankees and the Boston Red Sox, batting right-handed or left-handed for each player, imagining himself coming up in game situations and booming hits into the farthest corners of Yankee Stadium and Fenway Park.

Twenty years later, in 1967, playing left field for the Boston Red Sox, Carl Yastrzemski had the rare pleasure of making all those boyhood dreams of glory come true. In that year, the Red Sox, rated a 100-1 shot after a ninth-place finish in 1966, became the "miracle team" that won the most exciting pennant race in modern baseball history — and it was the heroics of Carl Yastrzemski, his clutch hits and brilliant fielding in game after game, that made this victory possible.

Perhaps no other ballplayer has ever had as brilliant a single year as Yastrzemski did in 1967. It was not simply that he won a Triple Crown with 44 home runs (he tied the Minnesota Twins' Harmon Killebrew), 121 runs batted in and a .326 average. It was the way he came through time after time to save or win a game for the Red Sox.

As the season progressed and the Red Sox stayed locked in a four-cornered race with the Chicago White Sox, the Detroit Tigers and the Minnesota Twins, the victory-hungry fans of Boston and New England began to believe that the impossible was going to happen. At every turn, Yastrzemski fueled that faith with his heroics, and as the pressure mounted, his efficiency went up with it. In Boston's last 12 games, he hit five homers, drove in 16 runs, scored 14 and averaged .523.

The entire season finally came down to the last two games. With Chicago out of the race, Boston and Detroit both trailed Minnesota by one game. Boston had two single games against Minnesota in Boston. Detroit played two doubleheaders against the California Angels in Detroit. If Boston won two and Detroit lost three, Boston would take the pennant.

On Saturday, Detroit lost and Boston beat the Twins 6-4. Yastrzemski hit two singles in his first three times at bat, the second driving in a run. When he batted in the seventh against Jim Merritt, there were two men on base and Boston was leading 3-2. The count went to 3 balls, 1 strike. Yaz looked for a fastball, and when it came in he sent it sailing into the right field bleachers. Killebrew cut the Boston lead to 6-4 with his 44th homer, tying Yaz, but Boston hung on to win. Now they were tied for first place with Minnesota, with Detroit half a game back.

The last game, the money game. Yastrzemski got a single and double his first two turns at bat, but Minnesota led 2-0 as Yaz made one of his rare errors to let one run score. In the fifth, he came up with the bases loaded and banged a single over second to drive in two runs and tie the score. Boston got three more in that inning and led 5-2 going into the eighth.

One more great play from Yaz. With two men on in the eighth, Minnesota's Bob Allison hit a ball into the left field corner. It could have been a double that would score two runs, but Yastrzemski played the ball perfectly, cutting it off before it hit the wall. Then he unleashed a throw to second that caught Allison by 20 feet. That was the ball game, 5-3. When Detroit lost the second game of its doubleheader to California, a few hours later, the Red Sox were the American League champs. In the two games against Minnesota, Yastrzemski had seven hits in eight times at bat.

The Red Sox lost the Series to the St. Louis Cardinals in seven games, but not because Yaz

"Yaz" delights fans with mighty swing.

to college and that he receive at least a $100,000 bonus. Carl finally signed with the Red Sox when he was 19 and a sophomore at Notre Dame. Deciding that he would finish college while playing baseball, he spent two years in the minors, 1959 at Raleigh, in the Class B Carolina League, where he hit .377, and 1960 at Minneapolis in the American Association, where he hit .342.

He came up to the Red Sox in 1961 and three years later, in 1963, he won his first batting title, with a .321 average. That was a prelude to his fantastic performance in 1967. In 1968 he went on to hit .301, which gave him his third batting title. That, he said, was a "lucky break." He was the only hitter in the league to go above .300 in a year when pitchers had the upper hand.

In 1970, Yaz came heartbreakingly close to his fourth American League batting title, a feat accomplished only by Ty Cobb, Harry Heilmann and Ted Williams. Yaz finished the season at .3286. Alex Johnson of the California Angels won the crown with an average of .3289.

An intense competitor, Yas swings so hard at times that his helmet comes off and he ends up on his knees. He's not big at 5'11", 180 pounds, however, and his power comes from perfect timing. "I have the type of swing," he says, "that if I am a little off in my balance I will be awful. I'm a streaky hitter for this reason." In 1970, for example, he was hitting .268 at the end of June Then he started on a hot streak and banged out hits at a terrific pace. Over the next six weeks, he hit .414, had 14 home runs and 37 runs batted in. In 1971, on the other hand, he was bothered by a hand injury, never got hot and fell off in all categories, ending the year with a .255 average, 15 home runs and 70 runs batted in.

Still, his 10 year average at the end of the '71 season was .296, and he had a total of 242 homers and 869 runs batted in. One of baseball's great hitters, he is one of its best fielders as well, both in the outfield and at first, which he played most of the 1970 season. He can, in fact, play any infield position and works out at third base nearly every day to keep his fielding at top level.

That is the kind of determination Carl Yastrzemski has always had. It carried him to super-stardom —and it will keep him there.

faltered. He had three home runs, hit .400 and starred defensively. But Bob Gibson beat Boston three times to carry the Cardinals to victory.

Among the honors he won in 1967, Yastrzemski was voted the American League's Most Valuable Player and awarded the $10,000 Hickok belt as the Professional Athlete of the Year.

Carl Yastrzemski had come a long way from the potato fields of Bridgehampton, where he was born in 1939 and where he grew up. But not without an enormous amount of hard work. Encouraged by his father to plan for a professional baseball career, Carl practiced relentlessly. When he made the Bridgehampton High School varsity as a 120-pound, 13-year-old, for example, and discovered that he was too weak to hit the pitching of 17-year-olds, he spent the next winter swinging a lead bat every evening in the freezing Yastrzemski barn. The next year he hit .650.

Word of Carl's talent spread, and major league scouts began to come around while he was still in high school. Carl, Sr. was determined that Carl go

Leroy Kelly

In his eight seasons as a running back for the Cleveland Browns, Leroy Kelly has gained more than 6000 yards, 6074 to be exact. Each time Kelly has cradled the ball in his arms and headed for the line of scrimmage, he's averaged more than four and one-half yards.

Kelly is now tenth on pro football's all-time rushing list, and number four on the touchdown-scoring list with 70, just behind Joe Perry with 71. Leading both lists is Jim Brown, Kelly's incomparable predecessor, whose totals of 12,312 yards rushing and 106 touchdowns may never be surpassed.

Jimmy Brown, of course, is a tough act to follow. There were those who said that Kelly was not equal to the task of replacing him when Brown retired just before the start of the 1966 season. Kelly, who was born in Philadelphia in 1942 and went to high school there, had been an eighth round draft choice in 1963 after playing college ball at Morgan State. In 1964 and 1965, he carried the ball just 43 times while Brown was finishing out his fabulous career. (He did see action as a punt returner and led the league in this department in 1965.)

But when Kelly stepped into the gap that Brown left in 1967, he proved immediately that he was right on top of the situation. He led the NFL in rushing in both 1967 and 1968, with 1205 yards in 1967 and 1239 in '68 and he registered a total of 26 touchdowns in those years. Not bad for the man who couldn't replace Brown. It is, in fact, safe to say that Kelly has been the player mainly responsible for the Browns winning either a conference or a division championship six of the last eight years.

Kelly is an interesting runner to watch. Like Brown, he is deceptive in many ways. After a tackle, Brown used to love to walk back to the huddle as slowly as a man heading for his own execution, looking as if some vital part of him had been destroyed when he'd been hurled to the ground. On the next play, Brown was as full of force and power as ever. Kelly, too, ambles slowly about the field—except of course when he gets the ball.

Beyond that, Kelly's running style is itself deceptive. He's not a straight ahead power runner by any means. Nor is he particularly "fancy." The key to his running style is intelligence. Kelly has a marvelous ability to use his blockers well. He also has an instinctive sense of how a play is unfolding, where the key defensemen are going. He uses this instinct to squeeze every available yard out of a running play. Another of Kelly's assets is that he runs flatfooted, which gives him good traction on all kinds of fields. And, finally, he gets off to an incredibly fast start—on hard fields or sloppy ones.

Despite his league-leading rushing total, Kelly's performance has been greatly hampered by injuries. In comparison to what he did in 1967 and 1968, Kelly had disappointing seasons in 1969 and 1970 because he was hurt. In 1970, for example, he had a couple of sprained ankles and a strained Achilles tendon as well. "Leroy wasn't better than 80 per cent most of the season," the Browns' coach, Nick Skorich, said. "The injuries affected his quick moves when openings occurred on the line. They also affected his pass patterns, the quick breaks into the secondary and his blocking on sweeps." His rushing total of 656 in 1970 was his lowest figure since he replaced Brown. Still, it was good enough for eighth place in the conference and, in addition, Kelly gained over 300 yards on pass receptions.

And even with his injuries, Kelly had some sensational days in 1970. One of these came in a game with the Houston Oilers in December. The Browns needed this game badly to regain a tie for the lead in the American Football Conference's Central Division.

As usual Kelly came through again in the clutch, gaining 108 yards on 20 carries and scoring a touchdown on a one-yard sweep around right end. The touchdown that put Cleveland ahead for good came with only eight seconds left in the first half, and the big gain in Cleveland's 99-yard drive to the goal line was Kelly's 32-yard run up the middle from his own four yard line.

In 1971 Kelly again lifted his performance to a superlative level when it counted most and again was largely responsible for bringing the Browns the Central Division title. Neither Kelly nor the Browns showed very much at the beginning of the season, and at one point the team lost four straight games. Still, they came down to the wire with a chance to win the title. Kelly came into the decisive game against the Cincinnati Bengals with 100-plus-yard performances in the previous two games.

Against the Bengals, he racked up 127 yards, mainly on sweeps and traps. It was the old Kelly of 1967 and 1968 back in action again—fast, sure-footed and tough to handle. The decisive touchdown came in the fourth quarter on an 80-yard drive, and Kelly was the big man for the Browns in bringing the ball down the field. During the drive the Browns didn't throw a single pass and Kelly finally took the ball over from the four yard line to give Cleveland a 31-27 victory.

"Leroy did the job," Bill Nelsen, the Browns quarterback, said after the game.

Doing the job, in fact, is what Kelly's career has been all about and he's done it not only as a runner but as a blocker, pass receiver and punt returner. There are those who say that Kelly is at the end of his career, that the years ahead are bound to be downhill for him because of his relatively small size, that the backs of the future are the big boys, like Larry Csonka of the Miami Dolphins and Norm Bulaich of the Baltimore Colts, both a good deal larger than Kelly.

The reason this is true, they say, is that the defense has changed considerably since Kelly broke into the game. The change began when the American Football League merged with the NFL, bringing into popularity what is called the "stacked defense." In this defense the defending linemen move toward the side of the field where there is the most running space, the wide side. This means that the defensive tackle plays in front of the offensive center, who is therefore no longer as free to make a slant block or go out after a linebacker. Blocking assignments of the other offensive linemen are more difficult as well. The net result is that it's far tougher for the offensive team to run end sweeps—and the sweep, of course, is Kelly's patented play.

But Kelly has never been a big man physically and his relatively small size did not prevent him from becoming a superstar in the first place. What he takes on the field besides his size is competitive desire, football intelligence, and his marvelous talents. Kelly is aware of the possible effect of the stacked defense on his running capacity. He admits, in fact, that it has made sweeps a lot more difficult to run. "But," he says, "when they stack up to cut off the sweep they've got to leave weaknesses somewhere, and we'll be coming up with plays to take advantage of those weaknesses."

Kelly has always responded to challenges. Anyone asked to fill Jim Brown's shoes would have to. It seems likely that in this case, too, Kelly will rise to the occasion. In any event, he says, "I honestly believe there is still a place in the game for a back my size. I'm looking forward to the challenge. Definitely."

Gordie Howe

To his Detroit Red Wing teammates, Gordie Howe was always the "big guy." Not just because he was physically big and tough but because, with amazing consistency, he came through with the big play, the vital goal, the super move that turned a game around. Howe is, in fact, the best all-around player in the history of the game, and when he retired in 1971 at the age of 43 after 25 seasons, he owned the most fantastic collection of records any hockey player has ever produced.

Howe was a lot less colorful and flamboyant than the two men with whom he is often compared, Maurice "The Rocket" Richard and Bobby Hull, whose headlong scoring dashes down the ice lifted fans out of their seats. Howe didn't generate great bursts of skating speed as they did nor did he get off their sensational shots. Howe's style, his way of making everything he did on the ice look easy, served to mask his extraordinary talents.

Howe's skill as a player was built, first of all, on his enormous strength. Six feet, 205 pounds, with a 17-inch neck, powerful, sloping shoulders and long arms with steampipe-thick wrists, Howe could get off a shot — and score — with two or three men crowding him out of a play.

His teammates called him "power" — with good reason. Bobby Hull, acknowledged to have the fastest slap shot in hockey, hits it at 118 miles an hour. A slap shot takes a determined wind-up. Howe's wrist shot — no wind-up — came sizzling in at 114 miles an hour. Howe's shot was, besides, the most accurate in the NHL, and since he was the only truly ambidextrous player in hockey, he could get it off with equal devastation from either side of his body.

Howe played with a 21-ounce stick made of Canadian ash with an extremely stiff handle. Detroit Red Wing trainer Lefty Wilson noted that Howe was likely to break an ordinarily flexible stick "like a toothpick. He is so strong," Wilson said, "that when he shoots the handle bends like a banana."

Howe used his strength to maximum advantage. Players who fouled him, anyone who tried to stop him physically, always got back more punishment than they gave out.

His success can be measured in the statistics. To begin with, Howe scored more goals than any other player, 786. Maurice Richard retired with a total of 544 after his nineteenth season. At the start of the 1971-72 season, his fifteenth, Bobby Hull led all other players with 554. So it's likely that Howe's record will stand for some years to come.

Howe's second amazing mark is his point total of 1809, the sum of goals scored and assists. Howe averaged an incredible 40 assists per year, and his total of 954 leads the runner-up, Red Winger Alex Delvecchio, by more than 300, Hull by more than 500, Richard by more than 600.

What these figures mean, quite simply, is that Howe is the most productive goal-scorer and assist-maker hockey has ever known. And playing longer than anyone else (he holds the record for most games played) Howe never let up. In his last full season, 1970-71, despite an arthritic wrist and elbow and a full month out of action with a torn cartilage in his rib cage, he scored 23 goals and 29 assists for 52 points — more points than he had in each of his first three seasons.

Gordie Howe came up to the NHL in 1946 after a year with Detroit's farm club at Omaha, a shy, anxious-to-please 18-year-old from Floral, Sas-

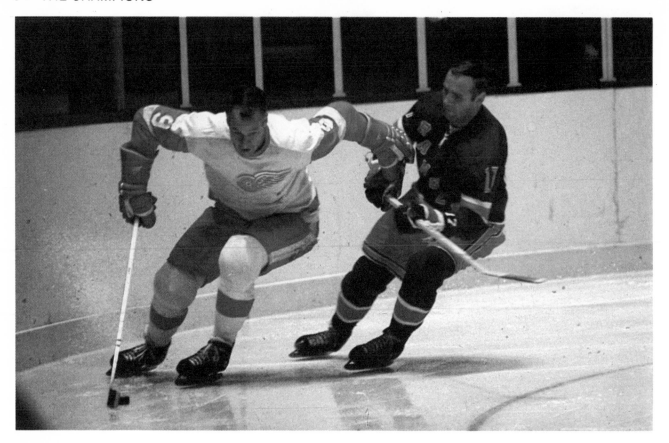

Howe *(left)*, "The Big Guy," uses great strength to control puck in game with Rangers.

katchewan. "I'm really just a lucky old farm boy," Howe says. "I remember when I came up, I cut out all the newspaper pictures showing me in a Red Wing uniform just to prove to everyone that I played in the NHL."

Like many Canadian boys, Gordie spent a good part of his boyhood on skates. He skated to school on the rivers and ponds that marked the way, and when he got home his mother spread newspapers in the kitchen so that he wouldn't have to take his skates off before he went out to play hockey.

From the beginning, Howe had one quality that brought his talent and physical strength into sharp focus: a soaring determination to play well. "Gordie Howe has simply got to be first," says Doug Roberts, a former teammate. "Even in practice you take the puck away from Gordie Howe and you'd better be ready for some sore wrists...."

Howe was playing right wing as hard in his last seasons as he did at 18. In a game between Detroit and the Toronto Maple Leafs in the 1969 season, Howe demonstrated his fantastic skills and desire once again. It was the season's opener for Detroit,

and they were ahead 3-1 in the third period.

Over the blue line on a breakaway dash with the puck came Toronto's Wayne Carleton. There was no one between him and Detroit's goalie, Roy Edwards. The only man near him was Howe. Since the 41-year-old veteran was behind Carleton, since Carleton had a speeding start, since the ice was soft and slow, it was highly unlikely that Howe could catch the 23-year-old Maple Leaf. And yet, before Carleton had taken 10 strides, Howe was up to him. His stick moved out and caught Carleton under the arm, a penalty maneuver, but one that neatly stopped Carleton from taking any kind of strong shot. Howe's move may have saved Detroit's victory, for the final score was 3-2 and the Maple Leafs were coming on hard at the end.

If any further proof is needed of Howe's value to Detroit over his 25-year career, here is one more statistic: over a 20-year period, from 1950 through 1969, Howe scored or assisted on one out of every three Red Wing goals. As Frank Selke Sr., general manager of the Canadiens when Richard played for them, has said: "If I want a perfect type of player, I would have to pick Howe."

■

Tom Seaver

When 22-year-old Tom Seaver, boyish-looking and chubby-cheeked, reported to the New York Mets training camp in St. Petersburg, Florida, in the spring of 1967, he brought with him one year of minor league experience, a strong right arm and an almost childlike belief in the joy and necessity of winning.

It was this last quality which should have given him the most trouble. In their five years of existence, the Mets were a team that had developed an almost magical ability to play badly. As thousands of loyal, resigned and often amused Shea Stadium regulars could testify, if there was a bonehead play to be made, the Mets would make it—and find a new and zany way to do it, besides. "Can't anyone here play this game?" asked Casey Stengel during his four years as the team's manager.

The perfection of the Mets' ineptitude was comical, of course, and much worse, hopeless—or so it seemed. The Mets' way was certainly not the way that George Thomas Seaver, born in 1944 in Fresno, California, and positive that he would grow up to be a major league baseball player, felt about the game. Seaver says: "The happiness of baseball is its competitiveness; that is what I love about the game." Competing, of course, means trying to win. That was the revolutionary ideal that Tom Seaver brought to the downtrodden Mets.

Seaver came to the Mets in a roundabout way. He was drafted by the Dodgers while he was attending the University of Southern California. He'd gone to college in the hope that this would happen; if he got a major league offer, he would quit school and finish his education in the off-season. He refused the Dodgers, however, because they didn't offer enough money. Then he accepted a $40,000 offer from the Atlanta Braves, only to have the baseball commissioner void it because of an irregularity. Finally, bid for by four teams, he went to the Mets when the commissioner pulled their name out of a hat in the spring of 1965.

He spent the 1966 season at the Mets' highest farm team, Jacksonville, Florida. He was obviously "special." The question was, how fast would he move up? At Jacksonville, he had a 12-12 record, and the Mets decided to take a look at him in the spring of 1967. He impressed manager Wes Westrum and pitching coach Rube Walker enough to make the team. Walker recalls: "He had more natural talent than any rookie I had ever seen, and I kept thinking 'he can't be this good.' But he was, he really was."

Seaver, the youngest of four children, came from an athletic family. His father was an outstanding golfer and played football and basketball as well at Stanford University. Tom played Little League baseball and starred for Fresno High School. "Our family was always competitive," Seaver says. "Even when my father was working around the house, he wanted perfection, and he tried to instill that striving in us, too."

His first season on the Mets, helped by Rube Walker, who sharpened up his curve and changeup, Seaver had a 16-13 record, 170 strikeouts, a 2.76 earned run average. Seven of his losses were by one run. Amazing statistics for a pitcher on a team that finished the season in tenth place with a 61-101 record, and it was not surprising that he was named Rookie of the Year.

But there was still the Met team, going nowhere. Their 1966 record was better than what they had done in 1962, their first year, when they lost 120 out of 160 games. But not that much better. And what bothered Tom Seaver was that the players seemed to be resigned to their fate as "losers." "There was an aura of defeatism on the team," Seaver has said, "and I refused to accept it. The lovable loser stuff was not funny to me."

In 1968, the Mets got a new manager, Gil Hodges, who'd previously played for them. And in 1968, the Mets began to win. With Jerry Koosman, Nolan Ryan and Tug McGraw, among others, holding up the pitching end along with Seaver, and with leftfielder Cleon Jones and centerfielder Tommie Agee contributing at bat, the Mets won 73 games in 1968 and finished just eight games short of the .500 mark—a new high for the "lowlies." Seaver had another good year to lead the way, a 16-12 record, 205 strikeouts and a 2.20 ERA.

His teammates came to respect and admire Seaver's desire to be the best, to compete and win. He was, clearly, the team's leader. All who observed him, as a player and as a person, came away impressed with his talent, maturity and competitive desire. Gil Hodges said: "I couldn't believe his maturity. I knew he'd be my team leader, and I knew he'd be the pitcher everyone said he'd be. He wanted it badly enough to work for it." And his desire rubbed off on the others.

So 1969 came, the magic year that turned the Met frogs into princes. If luck and fate had something to do with the Mets' first place finish, talent had as much, for under Hodges the Mets became a solid, well-managed team with strength all down the line and, first and foremost, a superlative pitching staff. Still, the way the Mets won it made their victory seem all the more magical. On August 15, they were nine and one-half games behind the eastern division leaders, the Chicago Cubs. A month later, after a 26-7 winning stretch, they were three and one-half games in front. On September 24, Gary Gentry beat the St. Louis Cardinals and the Mets clinched the eastern division title. They ended up eight games in front of the Cubs, and won 38 of their last 48 games.

Along the way, there was the magic—clutch hits, brilliant fielding plays. And there was solid talent coming through. Gil Hodges made all the right moves. Agee and Jones had terrific years at bat.

And Seaver produced his most brilliant season, all the more valuable to the Mets because, in the do-or-die days of August and September, he was unbeatable, winning every game he pitched after August 5. He finished the season with a 25-7 record, leading the major leagues in victories and percentage. He had a 2.21 earned run average, 208 strikeouts in 272 innings and was voted the Cy Young Award as the National League's most outstanding pitcher.

His most brilliant performance came against the Cubs on the night of July 9. With one out in the ninth inning, he had a perfect game. Then a .243 hitter named Jimmy Qualls slashed a single into left center field. Seaver got the next two men

to register a one-hitter and beat the Chicago Cubs 4-0. After the game, he said: "I've never been so disappointed in my life. But we won the game and we're going to win the pennant." It was a good call.

Winning the pennant could easily have been triumph enough. But the Mets kept their momentum going by beating the western division winners, the Atlanta Braves, in three straight games. Seaver got them off on the right foot by winning the first one. When they took on Baltimore in the World Series, they were primed for victory.

It came in five games to make the dream complete. Baltimore won the first one. But New York came back to take the next two. The fourth game was played in Shea Stadium, with Seaver pitching for the Mets. The game came down to the ninth inning with New York leading 1-0. Then Seaver tired. The Orioles put men on first and third with one out. Brooks Robinson came to bat and hit a liner into the gap between right and center field. Ron Swoboda raced into the hole, dove at the ball. Tumbling over, he came to his feet waving his glove at the umpire to show he'd made the catch— a remarkable catch. One run scored and the game was tied 1-1. But Seaver got the next man, then set down the Orioles in the tenth. The Mets scored one run in the bottom of the tenth—on a pop fly double and a misplayed bunt. Someone up there liked New York, and the Mets took the next two games to win the Series. Casey said it: "Amazin'."

Though the Mets have not hit the top again, Seaver has continued to pitch superlatively. He was 18-12 in 1970, tailing off badly at the end of the season after having a 17-6 record. He felt that one reason for his disappointing finish (he won just one game out of the Mets' final 50) was that he had decided to pitch with three days' rest instead of four. Following this diagnosis, he came back super-strong in 1971, to compile a 20-10 mark, with a 1.76 earned run average, the league's lowest, and 295 strikeouts, highest number ever in the National League.

In five seasons, Seaver has now won 95 games and lost 54, and he is almost certain to end his career as a 300 game winner, which would put him in excellent company on the all-time winning list. As Tom Seaver says: "I never did find defeat particularly amusing."

Merlin Olsen

Merlin Olsen, the Los Angeles Rams' huge defensive tackle, knows exactly what he wants to do on a football field. Olsen says: "Our job is to destroy the offense, crush the passer, foul up their blocking and timing. I don't think hate before a game. With me it's pride. I don't want anyone to play better than me. If I play bad, I'm truly embarrassed."

Merlin Olsen plays well enough to be rated among the game's best. Norm Van Brocklin, coach of the Minnesota Vikings, a man not known to go out on a limb, thinks that Olsen is "the greatest tackle ever to have played the game."

Various offensive linemen around the league who've tried to contain Merlin Olsen's powerful charge also think he's pretty good. Gene Hickman, the Cleveland Browns' all-pro guard, played opposite Olsen in a Pro Bowl game and commented: "There is no way I can handle Olsen. No matter how I try to block him he still keeps coming. He's too strong and too quick."

San Diego's Walt Sweeney, also an all-pro guard, who was a first-round draft choice in 1963, says: "Olsen has to be the best defensive tackle there is. He has all the physical attributes and he's smart, besides. You can't outguess him. You might try with some other players. Like some guy will almost always come outside you, others almost always stay inside. You can anticipate. But it's impossible to anticipate what Olsen is going to do."

Olsen was regarded as outstanding as soon as he came into the league, the Rams' first-round draft choice in 1962. The following year he made the All-NFL second team, and since 1966 he's been a unanimous choice for the All-NFL first team.

Born in 1940, Olsen grew up in Logan, Utah, one of a family of nine children. He played football for Logan High School and then went on to Utah State, where he was named to every All-American team. He may be the start of a new super-breed, since he has two brothers who are as big—Phil, a defensive lineman for the Rams, and Orrin, who, it is said, is still growing and at 18 is 6'3" and 225 pounds.

Olsen's size—he's 6'5", 270 pounds—is of course an advantage to a man whose primary job is the pass rush. Watching Olsen bear down on him is not an occupation calculated to soothe a quarterback's nerves. And there's the further problem of trying to throw a football over Olsen's upstretched arms, a feat roughly comparable to throwing a stone over the Washington Monument.

Olsen's theory on pass rushing is fairly elementary—not that it doesn't get results. "You must keep coming," he says. This basic theory applies whether the quarterback is a fast-throwing one like Jon Brodie of the San Francisco 49ers or one who likes to hold on to the football while he looks for the long pass, like Daryl Lamonica of the Oakland Raiders. The tackle's job is the same in both cases, Olsen feels. It's not just dumping the quarterback that counts. It's establishing what might be called "a regime of terror" in which the quarterback is continually hurried and harrassed. "We've got to make the quarterback throw before he wants to," Olsen says. "That's the key."

One quarterback for whom Olsen has a good deal of respect is the 49ers' Brodie, a man he's faced more than 30 times. "When he's hot," Olsen says, "Brodie is the best we see." The Rams have, over the years, not been particularly successful in intimidating or "sacking" Brodie, at least not as successful as they've been in menacing other quarterbacks in the league. One reason for this, Olsen believes, is that the 49ers have a strong offensive line. Besides that, though, Olsen thinks that Brodie himself has had a lot to do with it. "It shows," Olsen says, "that his play selection is good and that he throws the ball fast."

Olsen plays alongside of another all-pro, David "Deacon" Jones, perhaps the top defensive end in the league. Merlin and Jones make the Ram's left side defensive line a nightmare for opposing quarterbacks, and the rush they can mount is awesome to behold. Beyond that, of course, they are equally tough on the run.

Olsen had a super year in 1969, as he and the Rams led the league in the number of times they dumped the opposing passer with an imposing total of 53, and he was named by his teammates as the club's most valuable player.

As big as he is, Olsen has not been immune to

Olsen (*right*) is rated among top tackles.

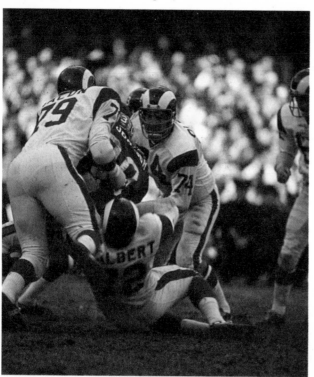

injury. In fact, at the end of the 1970 season, he suffered such serious damage to his right knee in a game against the Detroit Lions that for a while it seemed possible his playing career was over. But Olsen is tough as well as large and even with the injury he insisted on playing in the Rams' last contest of the season against the New York Giants. He might easily have sat the game out. Instead, he helped the Rams overwhelm New York 31-3 and played a slam-bang game in the process.

Olsen came back strong in 1971, even though his recovery from the operation on his injured knee kept him out of the exhibition season. In a game against Detroit, for example, Merlin and the rest of Los Angeles' "Fearsome Four," including his brother Phil at right tackle, almost set up housekeeping in the Detroit backfield. They sacked Detroit quarterback Greg Landry seven times in the course of the afternoon. Los Angeles won the game 21-13, and the general conclusion was that the defense had been mainly responsible. "We made the big plays," Merlin said after the game.

At 31 Olsen is at the point in his career and his life when he's begun to think about what he might do instead of playing football. He loves to hunt and fish and one of the things he complains about, only half-seriously, is that the best hunting and fishing are in the fall, when he's on a football field. And he's developed any number of off-season activities which could become full-time ones if he retired from the game.

But the Rams have not won a championship since 1955. Now their long-time coach, George Allen, is gone, replaced by former UCLA coach Tommy Prothro. Inevitably, Olsen and his teammates are wondering whether their luck will change and they'll find a Super Bowl in their future. That's something that Olsen would dearly love to experience, of course. So the chances are that he'll be around for a while. Despite his longing to go off hunting and fishing in the fall, Olsen really loves football. And he likes it best when the pressure is strongest. "I play better when things are going badly," he says. "I don't know why—I suppose it has something to do with the way I'm put together. The tougher things are, the more I enjoy football."

Pete Maravich

Pete Maravich can do amazing, magical things with a basketball. For example, the "walking pretzel," a warm-up exercise in which he passes a ball between his legs in a figure-eight movement. He can do this, as he says, "faster than the eye can see," and it is just one of a dozen or so patented, fantastic drills that Maravich has invented and loves to perform, especially in front of crowds.

He can do the "ricochet," the "running pretzel" and the "dribbling pretzel." He can "punch the bag," dribbling the ball one-eighth of an inch off the floor "so fast he can't even hear it hit." He can spin a ball on his finger for 30 minutes, flick it behind his back and catch it one one finger again.

And as dazzling as Maravich is in pre-game drills, he is just as dazzling in a game. As a pro, playing for the Atlanta Hawks, he has stopped using some of the more flamboyant of his passes and shots, adjusting his style to the team's. But he is still the most exciting player in the country.

In high school, and at Louisiana State University, Maravich made every game a theatrical event, an astounding exhibition of razzle-dazzle passing and shot-making that left fans roaring with delight and opposing players wondering what he ate for breakfast. Maravich was inevitably the star performer and, as such, free to do pretty much what he wanted. And what he wanted was to "put on a show." As he's said: "The audience has always been one of the most important parts of basketball to me."

To please crowds, Maravich never missed an opportunity to display his extraordinary bag of basketball tricks. He threw blind hook passes. He zipped the ball between an opposing player's legs on breakneck drives down the court. He unleashed behind-his-neck flips, tossed the ball around his body a full 180 degrees. Sometimes his passes were so magical they fooled his teammates. But mostly, he hit his man. And his shots were almost as innovative. Forty-foot push shots, spinning hooks, acro-batic delay layups—he threw the ball in from all over the court. In his senior year at LSU, he broke Oscar Robertson's collegiate scoring record of 2973 with 3590 points. He hit 69 points in one game, made more than 50 in 26 others. His floppy hair bouncing, his floppy gray socks (worn for luck) drooping at his ankles, 6′6″ and bone-thin at 180 pounds, Maravich drew huge crowds wherever he played, and for every crowd he "did his thing."

Pete Maravich started doing his tricks when he was seven years old. He was living in Clemson, South Carolina, where he grew up. His father, Press, had been an early pro basketball star for the Pittsburgh Iron Men, and then became a basketball coach. So Pete's interest in the game was natural.

Pete spent hours practicing each day. He'd walk the two miles from his house into Clemson dribbling all the way. When he went to the movies, his basketball went with him, and he sat in an end seat, so he could dribble on the aisle carpet while he watched. Practicing all alone in the gym, becoming bored with "just" dribbling and making baskets, he began to do "funny things" with the basketball, inventing wild ways to dribble and shoot.

In junior high and high school, he went on to do his "funny things" in games, and he was so delighted with the crowds' reaction that he worked on new tricks. At the same time, he was scoring points, averaging 32 a game in his senior year at Needham Broughton High School in Raleigh, North Carolina, where his father was coach at North Carolina State. Pete went on for a year of prep school. Then Press Maravich decided to take the coaching job at LSU, whose basketball team had been a weak one for years, and Pete went along. The idea was that together father and son would bring LSU back as a basketball power.

In his first year at LSU in 1966, Maravich led the freshman team through a season in which they lost just one game, while the varsity was winning only three. Often there were more fans watching Maravich play with the freshman team than there were watching the varsity. As a sophomore Maravich averaged 43.8 points a game, made every All-American team and brought LSU back to a respectable 14-12 record.

In addition, he became, almost overnight, a national phenomenon. He was, basically, the entire LSU offense, and opponents began to use the zone against him or if they played man-to-man, they fell off against Maravich so that often it seemed that five opposition players were guarding him. One former LSU star, watching other teams gang up on Maravich said: "Just once I would love to see a team play this guy honest. Pistol Pete would be so great that night, he'd scare people."

Maravich ended his sophomore year as the highest per-game scorer in collegiate history.

In his junior year his average went up to 44.2. He wasn't a perfect player by any means. He took wild shots, threw wild passes trying to please the crowd. But he scored and he led LSU to a winning season.

Between his junior and senior years, Maravich put on 20 pounds and felt that the added weight made him quicker as well as stronger. Whether or not the weight made a difference, Maravich led LSU to a 20-8 record as a senior against a very tough schedule that included Southern Cal, Oregon State and UCLA. His season average went higher, to 46.6 and Oscar Robertson's record fell along the way.

Now the big question became, which pro team would sign Maravich and how much money would he get. The answers, early in 1970, turned out to be: the Atlanta Hawks and close to two million dollars (the exact amount was not disclosed). Maravich's next goal, as he told a friend, was "to help win an NBA championship."

His first pro game with the Hawks was, fittingly enough, against the Milwaukee Bucks and Oscar Robertson. Interest in the game was high and ABC television paid $75,000 for the rights to televise the game — but only if Maravich played. It was not an auspicious debut for the "Pistol." He came into the game at the start of the second period, hit on a jump shot and a breakaway layup, but then did little, finishing with just seven points.

That game was an indication that, as great as Maravich had been in college, there would be a period of adjustment for him before he reached the stature he was capable of as a pro. To begin with, there were some problems. For one thing, his high salary caused resentment among some Hawks. For another, no man can dominate a pro team to the extent that Maravich dominated his college team. The players, his teammates and the opposition, are all just too good. In professional basketball, the winning team has to be a *team*. As a pro, Maravich had to overcome some tendencies that worked against the necessary team play. He dribbled too much and forced shots, tried too much "funny stuff" that resulted in turnovers. But the talent was there, and he had some outstanding nights, scoring 40 points against the New York Knicks, 41 against Buffalo, many of his points coming on acrobatic Maravich moves.

Despite the pressure, despite his mistakes, Maravich finished the season with a 23.2 average and 1880 points, which made him the league's seventh leading scorer.

In the 1971-72 season, Maravich's problems continued. To start with, he came down with mononucleosis, which kept him out of action for a couple of months and left him below par when he started playing. Still, he had a 19.3 average, second on the Hawks to Lou Hudson's 24.7, and there was general agreement that he was playing a much sounder game, throwing the ball away less frequently and disciplining himself to make his shots work.

What his first two seasons have shown is that Maravich has the talent to become one of pro basketball's truly great players. His major problem will probably be defense, but he will improve in that area. And meanwhile, his offensive talents are outstanding. He's so fast, has such a quick first step, that it's almost impossible to stop his drives without fouling him — and Maravich converts fouls at an 80 per cent rate. With the bad moments of his first two years behind him, "Pistol Pete" Maravich is ready to step out and become "so great he'll scare people."

Willie Mays

"He plays the game as if it's fun." Walter Alston, manager of the Los Angeles Dodgers said it, echoing what millions of fans have felt watching Willie Mays play baseball.

Alston and the fans are right. To Willie Howard Mays, Jr., baseball has above all been fun. As a kid in Fairfield, Alabama, where he was born in 1931, and where he grew up, Mays played sandlot baseball day in and day out, encouraged in his passion for the sport by his father, who played semi-professional baseball with the Birmingham Black Barons.

"It was a big surprise to me," Willie said later, "when I found out they paid my father money for playing baseball. That seemed like the best idea anyone ever thought of."

Willie played with Black Barons, too, and when he was 19, the New York Giants signed him. He played in a class B league for a year, was moved up to Minneapolis in 1951, and after 35 games, with his batting average .477, the Giants called him up to New York. He was two weeks past his twentieth birthday, overawed by the city and by playing in the major leagues. His first 21 times at bat he managed just one hit. After a particularly bad day, when he'd failed at bat in a number of men-on-base situations, the Giants' manager, Leo Durocher, found him sitting in front of his locker, crying. "I can't hit big league pitching," he told Durocher. "You better send me back down."

Durocher put his arm around Mays and said: "Go home and get a good night's sleep. You're my centerfielder tomorrow and every day after that as long as I'm here."

The next day, facing the crafty Warren Spahn of the Milwaukee Braves, Mays hit one over the roof of the Polo Grounds. He was on his way after that, and when he discovered that he was making it in the major leagues, he started to have fun again.

In 1954, after two years in the Army, Mays had his first big season. He hit .345 and clouted 41 home runs, to lead the Giants to a pennant and a World Series victory in four straight games over the Cleveland Indians. He was voted the league's Most Valuable Player. Other great years followed. For 13 straight seasons, Willie never had less than 29 home runs, and in 1965 he reached his high with 52 while hitting .317 and batting in 112 runs. In that year, he was named the National League's Most Valuable Player for the second time.

At the end of the 1971 season, his lifetime batting average was .305, and he was second on the homer list with 646 (Hank Aaron passed him in the 1972 season). He was high up also on the all-time list in runs, hits, total bases and runs batted in.

Always, he was the clutch performer, always he gave his all, his "hustle" becoming legendary. While baseball was fun, it was also a passion with Mays, and he could not spare himself. In 1962, in fact, he collapsed on the field from exhaustion. And always, he played the game with his own special style. He was the "say, hey" kid, who ran out from under his hat as he roared down the baseline. He was the inimitable outfielder who made fans hold their breath with his "basket" catches, and delighted them by lobbing the ball back to the infield underhanded. He was the major league ballplayer who finished a double-header in the Polo Grounds and then went out to play stickball with kids, swinging a broomstick handle at a rubber ball with as much delight as he swung a baseball bat, and, as one of the players recalls, "he hit that rubber ball long."

Out of his passion for the game and his fantastic skill came a tremendously high level of excellence,

Mays, an all-time great in center field, does outstanding job at first base, too.

day after day. And then there were the peaks, the incredible, impossible plays that glitter in memory. There was his catch in the opening game of the 1954 World Series. The batter was the Indians' Vic Wertz. He boomed the pitch out into center field. Mays turned at the sound of the bat and raced toward the wall at the 460 foot mark. Without turning his head to look for the ball, he stuck his glove up at exactly the right moment and grabbed it. Then he made a prodigious throw back to the infield to hold the runners on base.

Again, against the Brooklyn Dodgers, Mays raced at top speed into right center field to make an unbelievable grab of a ball hit by Carl Furillo. Billy Cox of the Dodgers was on third base and he tagged up to go home. Mays pulled the ball down going away from the plate. He knew the runner would go home, and instead of trying to stop, turn and throw, Mays caught it and in the very same motion pivoted in a counter-clockwise direction to rifle in a throw that reached the catcher at home plate without bouncing. Cox was out by 10 feet, and manager Charlie Dressen of the Dodgers was so unhappy he said: "Let's see him do it again." A less partisan reaction came from a sportswriter

who told Leo Durocher that he'd never seen a better play. "He does it every day," Durocher said.

Mays was of course capable of doing it again, and over the course of his career, he came up with any number of dazzling plays. As one sports writer noted, Mays had a "flair for heroics." In 1971, for example, slowed a step or two and tired from a long season, the 40 year-old Mays still gave his all down to the last day. In the playoff against Pittsburgh, which the Giants lost, he hit a double in the first game, a homer in the second. In the third, he banged out a single to left, then stole second. He wanted that one, wanted to appear in a fourth World Series before he retired. He didn't get it.

But the heroics continue. Traded to the Mets at the beginning of the 1972 season, Willie won the very first game in which he appeared in a New York uniform, hitting a fifth inning home run that beat the Giants. Nothing could have been more symbolic of the way Mays plays baseball.

As Willie McCovey of the Giants said a few weeks later, when Mays again beat the Giants with a homer: "Certain guys are just able to rise to the occasion. A tense situation might bother a lot of guys. But that's where Mays is best."

Jerry West

Jerry West did not perform at his usual high level in the 1972 championship playoffs. He did top all players in assists with 44, to keep in step with his regular season showing as the league leader in this category. But, gripped by a slump, West shot just 99 points in the five-game matchup between the Los Angeles Lakers and the New York Knicks—far below the close to 30 point average that has given him the record of 4052 points in 136 playoff games.

Still, despite his poor shooting, West was wildly happy when the playoffs were over, with Los Angeles a 4-1 victor. "Right now," he said after the final game, "I feel like I'm eight feet tall."

West's happiness was understandable. The 1972 playoffs marked the eighth time in the past 11 years that the Lakers had reached the final round of the playoffs. Most important to West and the other Lakers, it was the first time they had won.

Probably the most frustrating of those seven defeats for West had come in 1969, when the Boston Celtics, who finished fourth in the NBA's eastern division, beat the favored Lakers, who finished first in the west, in seven games. That was the playoff in which West gave what has been described as "the greatest playoff performance in history."

In the seventh game, despite a pulled hamstring muscle suffered in game number five, West was again brilliant. But Boston, led by John Havlicek, won the game 108-106 to take the title.

Not, however, without a last ditch effort by Jerry West, injured thigh and all. With nine minutes to go, the Celtics were leading by 17 points. West's thigh was heavily taped to give his leg support, but he still limped noticeably. Yet, in those final minutes, he put on a fantastic spurt, scoring 14 of the Lakers' 19 points, charging all over the court with demonic energy. He ended the game with 42 points and 12 assists. It wasn't enough.

West was named the outstanding player in the series by *Sport* magazine. In the five games before he hurt his leg, West had scored 53, 41, 24, 40 and 39 points, and he was all over the floor for the Lakers. Bill Russell called his performance in the first game, which the Lakers won, 120-118, "the greatest clutch performance ever against the Celtics." Boston's Larry Siegfried said: "He is the master. They can talk about the others, build them up, but he is the one. He is the only guard."

These were nice tributes, and West was certainly appreciative of the car that went with the *Sport* magazine award. But what he really wanted was the title, and it began to look as if he and the Lakers would never get it.

Jerry West began playing for Los Angeles in the fall of 1960. Born in 1938 in Cabin Creek, West Virginia, he had played high school basketball and led his team to the state championship. Then he went on to West Virginia University, where he made All-American three times. In 1959, his junior year, West Virginia advanced to the finals of the NCAA championship. That was the beginning of West's frustration when it came to titles. Though he scored 28 points and was voted the tournament's Most Valuable Player, West Virginia lost in the final by one point to California.

When West joined the Lakers, he was playing under his old college coach, Fred Schaus, and in his second year, as West averaged better than 30 points a game, the Lakers advanced to the finals in the playoffs for the NBA title. Their opponent was the Celtics, and the series came down to the seventh game. The Lakers lost when a shot by Frank Selvy just missed, bouncing off the rim.

In 1963, 1965, 1966 and 1968, like a broken record, Los Angeles lost to the Celtics. In 1970, the script changed slightly. Los Angeles lost to the New York Knicks, though West sent the first game into overtime with a fantastic 63-foot shot that hit the rim, bounced up and in just as the buzzer sounded.

So there was reason enough for West's frustration. He has enormous pride, cares deeply about playing well. His regular season play was superlative, his stature in the league assured. On the basis of his 12 seasons with the Lakers, he is regarded, along with Oscar Robertson of the Milwaukee Bucks, as the premier guard in the league. He is admired and respected for the consistency and all-around excellence of his play, and particularly for his ability to come through in the clutch.

To begin with, he is a fabulous shooter. At the end of the 1970 season, he had 16,835 points, an average of 27.5 per game. He is regarded by many coaches and players in the league as the best shooter from 15 feet out and farther in the NBA.

At the same time, he's rated by many as a better defensive guard than Oscar Robertson. And, unusual for a shooter, he ranks high in assists each year. His average after the 1970 season was better than five a game.

At 6'3" and 185 pounds, he's not big, and the aggressive driving game he plays has brought him more than his share of injuries. Over the years, his nose has been broken several times, and just about every part of his body has been banged up, more or less seriously. In fact, his total points are all the more impressive because he's missed more than 125 games in his career, even though, as in the 1969 playoffs, he's played with severe injuries at times.

What remains as the most impressive aspect of West as a basketball player is his clutch play, which is held in awe by players and coaches in the NBA. Undoubtedly, his ability to do the job when the chips are down is fueled by his pride.

"I've reached a point," he says, "where nothing will satisfy me but the very best. I can only settle for that from myself. I used to think so much about scoring, but I'm just no longer interested in points. I want to be appreciated for being more than a shooter."

But basketball is a shooting game, and West still comes through in that department—and more often than anyone else in the league when the points are needed most desperately.

In the 1972 NBA All-Star game, for example, he did it again. In a typical West spurt in the fourth quarter, he stole or deflected the ball on five occasions and made a number of key baskets. Then, with the score tied and just one second to go, guarded closely by one of the best defensive players in the league, the Knick's Walt Frazier, West dribbled to the top of the key and put the ball in cleanly to give the West a 112-110 victory.

In view of his capacity for clutch heroics, it was ironic that when the NBA title finally came to the Lakers, it did so without the necessity for West to churn up his adrenalin and come on like a dead-eyed gangbuster. Without Willis Reed, New York lacked a big man who could handle Wilt Chamberlain around the basket. Jerry Lucas, who had a brilliant year playing center for the Knicks in place of the injured Reed, simply was not physically equipped to do the job.

Consequently, the Knicks were forced to pursue an outside shooting strategy. This worked fine in the first game, when they hit 72 per cent of their shots. But when Dave Debusschere injured his side late in the third game, the Knicks lost a good outside shooter, a top defensive player and a strong rebounder. And they were playing a team that had swept the opposition out of its way during the regular season. Well-coached by ex-Celtic guard Bill Sharman, the Lakers had set an NBA record by winning an incredible 33 straight games, and they had polished off a strong Milwaukee team in the previous round of the playoffs.

Los Angeles had a scare after the third game when Wilt discovered that he had sprained his wrist. But ice packs reduced the swelling overnight and Chamberlain played extremely well. With Wilt dominating the game, the Lakers actually had little trouble with the Knicks. And in the fourth and fifth games, Jerry West began to get his shooting eye back. In the fourth game he scored 28. In the fifth, driving to the basket frequently, he hit 23 and had nine assists as well.

So victory came to the Lakers. They were the NBA champs, the best team in the world. And after the game West could say, finally: "How do I feel? I feel eight feet tall."

Bob Gibson

On July 15, 1967, pitching against the Pittsburgh Pirates, Bob Gibson, the tall, hard-throwing St. Louis Cardinal righthander, was hit on the right shin by a blistering shot off the bat of the Pirates' rightfielder, Roberto Clemente. Gibson's leg hurt, but he thought it was just a bruise. He insisted on staying in the game. He pitched to two more men before his leg collapsed as he faced the third. At the hospital, X-rays showed that he had a broken leg.

Gibson's competitive spirit is highly developed, to say the least. He couldn't wait to get back in action, particularly since the Cardinals were heading for a pennant, and Gibson feels that winning a World Series game is the "ultimate achievement" for a pitcher. Gibson's record was 10-6 when he was hurt. He came back seven weeks later at the beginning of September and finished the season with a 13-7 record, pitching the pennant-clinching victory against the Philadelphia Phillies on September 18.

Led by Carl Yastrzemski, the Boston Red Sox had won the American League pennant. Cardinal manager Red Schoendienst could select his pitcher for the first game from a staff that included Nelson Briles (14-5), Steve Carlton (14-9) and Dick Hughes (16-6). Announcing that Gibson would face the Red Sox, Schoendienst said: "If you have a man with the ability of Bob Gibson, you have no choice but to give him the toughest job."

Gibson beat the Red Sox 2-1 in the first game, striking out 10. Then he gave the Cardinals a 3-1 lead in the Series by winning the fourth game 6-0 on a five-hitter. But Boston came back to take games number five and six, and Gibson took the mound again, with just three days' rest, in the decisive seventh game. He pitched a three-hitter, striking out 10, for a 7-2 win that gave the Cardinals the Series victory. Voted the Series' Most Valuable Player, Gibson also tied a record set by Christy Mathewson in 1905 by allowing just 14 hits in 27 innings.

That was the second time Bob Gibson had been named the Most Valuable Player in a World Series. The first was in 1964, when St. Louis beat the New York Yankees, also in seven games. Gibson won two of the three games he pitched that year, including the final one.

The Cardinals won the pennant again in 1968 as Gibson came through with a fantastic year. He had a 22-9 record, and his 1.12 earned run average was the lowest in that category in modern baseball history. In one stretch, he won 15 straight games and registered a string of 45 scoreless innings. He led the league in strikeouts with 268 and pitched 13 shutouts. For this performance, he was named the league's Most Valuable Player. He also received the Cy Young Award.

In the first game of the 1968 Series, Gibson squared off against the Tigers' 31-game winner, Denny McLain. He not only beat McLain 4-0 on a five-hitter but struck out 17 to break Sandy Koufax's World Series strikeout record by two. He set another record by gaining his seventh consecutive Series victory in the fourth game. Once again the Series came down to the wire, however, and in the seventh game, hurt by a few Cardinal mistakes, Gibson finally lost. (But he set another Series record with 35 strikeouts in seven games.)

Bob Gibson's Series performance is one that no other active pitcher comes close to equalling. It reflects, as much as his natural talent, his intense desire to excel. Johnny Keane, the Cardinals' manager, paid tribute to this quality with a comment he made after the 1964 Series. In the seventh game, pitching with two days rest, Gibson tired. In the ninth inning, he gave up two Yankee homers to make the score an uncomfortably close 7-5. But Keane let him stay in, and Gibson got the side out for the win. Asked why he didn't send in a relief pitcher, Keane replied that Gibson had done a magnificent job for the Cardinals all season and deserved to finish the game. "I committed myself to his heart," the manager said.

Bob Gibson's teammates and the league's best hitters are equally aware of Gibson's "heart," his

Gibson's pitching won two World Series.

overpowering will to win. Now 36, and starting his fourteenth season with St. Louis in 1972, Bob Gibson took the long road to success as baseball's highest paid pitcher (his salary is $150,000 a year). He grew up in an Omaha ghetto, the youngest of seven children. His father died of pneumonia a month before he was born, his mother earned very little working as a cleaning woman. A frail child, Gibson almost died of pneumonia when he was three, and he suffered from rickets, asthma and a rheumatic heart as well. Once he was bitten by a rat as he slept.

Gibson was not allowed to try out for his high school baseball team because, the coach said, he reported one day too late. Gibson felt the color of his skin had something to do with it. But he did play basketball and won a scholarship to Creighton University in Omaha, after Indiana University, his first choice, rejected him because its "Negro quota" had been filled.

In college Gibson was an outstanding basketball player, and he starred in baseball, too, as a pitcher and outfielder. In 1957, six credits short of a degree, he signed with both the St. Louis Cardinals and the touring team of the Harlem Globetrotters. He would play basketball with the Globetrotters after the baseball season ended.

He soon quit the Globetrotters to concentrate on baseball as a pitcher. He was with the Omaha Cardinals in 1957 and Rochester in 1958. He came up to the Cardinals in the middle of 1959 and compiled an uninspired 2-5 record. He did not do particularly well in 1960, either. But he was learning a lot about pitching. In 1961, when Johnny Keane replaced Solly Hemus as the Cardinals' manager, he took Gibson aside and told him that he would be in the starting rotation. Keane had been Gibson's manager at Omaha, and with Keane's encouragement and guidance, Gibson had his first successful year, with a 13-12 record, 166 strikeouts and a 3.24 earned run average. In '62 he was 15-13 (he broke his leg late in the season) and in '63, 18-9. Then came the 1964 season, when Gibson had a 19-12 record and won nine of his last thirteen decisions, to lead the Cardinals to their first pennant since 1946.

St. Louis has not won a pennant since 1968, so Gibson has not had the opportunity to show his stuff in a World Series again. But he has continued to perform brilliantly in the regular season. In 1969, he won 20 games while losing 13. In 1970, he had a 23-7 record, led the major league in victories and was voted the Cy Young Award for the second time.

It was during the 1970 season that Red Schoendienst said: "I certainly don't want to take anything away from some of the pitchers I played with or against over the years, but Bob Gibson is the best pitcher I have ever seen."

In 1971, Gibson was out for three weeks with a torn thigh muscle and ended the season with a 16-13 record. But he pitched his first no-hitter, against the Pittsburgh Pirates on August 14.

Gibson himself feels he has another three or four seasons ahead of him. "I've got to do things differently now because I don't have the whoosh on my fastball," he says. "I may have lost about 10 per cent of velocity but what I'm missing in speed, I'll make up in know-how and effectiveness."

There aren't too many National League hitters who'll argue with Gibson on that score. As Willie Stargell, the Pirates' slugging outfielder, said after Gibson's no-hitter: "You can tell all of those people who've been saying Gibson is washed up that they should have been at the plate with a bat in their hands."

Phil Esposito

He's on the beefy side and he wouldn't get very far in a Mr. Muscles contest. He has bad feet, and when he skates down the ice he sometimes seems as clumsy as a man juggling one grocery bag too many. Never mind. Phil Esposito, the Boston Bruins' All-Star center has a few other things going for him. For one, he has turned hockey's scoring records upside down, first cracking the 100-points-in-a-season barrier, a level that seemed unattainable just a few years ago, and then going far beyond that to the 150 point level. Who would bet now that Phil Esposito will not push close to 200?

Esposito's scoring feats have been downgraded by some. They point out that Maurice Richard scored 50 goals, long the record, during a 50-game season, much shorter than the 78-game schedule that now prevails. They maintain that the expansion of the league has brought many players of sub-par caliber into the NHL. They say that the Boston Bruins are such a strong team it's easy for Esposito to score goals.

Esposito came to Boston in 1967 from the Chicago Black Hawks, where he centered on a line with Bobby Hull. The highest number of goals he scored as a Black Hawk was 27. Even then he was called a "garbage collector," to indicate that he got his goals by poking in other players' shots.

Criticism of Esposito is becoming more and more difficult, however, because he's turned into such a consistent and overpowering scorer. Beyond that, any number of people have maintained all along that Esposito's problem with his critics is his deceptiveness—starting with the fact that he doesn't look like a hockey player in the heroic, muscular mold of Bobby Hull and Gordie Howe.

Esposito's style is deceptive as well. On the ice, he seems to move slowly, to look as if he couldn't care less. His clumsy style actually masks the fact that he's an extremely fast skater. His legs don't pump as quickly as a shorter man's, but he covers a great deal of territory in a short amount of time with his long strides.

He's deceptive, too, when he moves down the ice with the puck. As his teammate, Ed Westfall has noted, "Espo shows the puck to the defenseman and he seems to be moving nice and slow. The next thing the guy knows, Phil is by him. Espo may look slow but he's so strong he'll beat the other guy by four or five feet."

Esposito's strength has a great deal to do with his success. He is capable of pushing a defenseman away with one hand while he skates right around him. The other key element in his ability to score is his quickness with a hockey stick. "He gets the puck and fires it into the goal while you're still trying to figure out how he got it in the first place," says Bruin Ed Johnston.

Esposito's favorite position is 10 or 15 feet from the goal mouth, a spot from which he can use his two greatest assets, his quick stick and his strength, to grab the puck and fire away. Since the Bruins are indeed loaded with good hockey players, if the opposition pays too much attention to Esposito, his linemates have a better chance to get open. And behind all this stands Bobby Orr, ready to shoot his bullets at the goal.

One other criticism of Esposito is that he's point-hungry, which hardly seems fair. After all, there aren't too many hockey players around who don't feel that scoring a goal is a nice way to go through a day. Certainly Esposito has always played a team game and often, as in the 1972 playoffs against the Rangers, when he doesn't score he still contributes strongly to the Bruins' attack.

Esposito himself answers his critics by saying: "We didn't set records because of weak opponents. We did it because of our overall offensive philosophy. We hit, we get in position in front of the net, we help each other."

Behind the argument, there stand, incontrovertible, the records in the book. In 1968-69 he scored 126 points on 49 goals and 77 assists. In 1970-71, after a 99 point season the preceding year, Espo moved up to 152, on 76 goals and 76 assists, breaking Bobby Hull's goal-scoring record of 58, set in 1968-69. And in 1971-72, Esposito weighed in with another blockbuster season, registering 66 goals and 68 assists for 133 points. In 1968-69, 1970-71 and 1971-72 he won the Art Ross Trophy as the league's scoring champion. His 66 goals in 1971 also tied Bobby Hull's record of having scored more than 50 goals in two consecutive seasons.

It all adds up to an unprecedented scoring spree. Playing with the Bruins has of course made a difference to Esposito. They are an awesome hockey team, and they've given Esposito the advantage of having extremely strong wings to help him out—among others, Ken Hodge and Wayne Cashman. But Esposito himself, in the eyes of many observers, has developed enormously as a center since coming to Boston. He's adapted his style to the Boston attack, taken good advantage of his scoring opportunities.

As Esposito says: "In Boston I'm carrying the puck more. In Chicago we gave it off to the wings. But my wings here are getting me the puck from the corner. A center can't ask for more."

Phil Esposito learned his hockey in the schoolboy and junior leagues of Canada, graduating to the Chicago Black Hawks in 1963. Born in Sault Ste. Marie, Ontario, in 1942, Phil used to get up at five o'clock in the morning so that he and his brother Tony could get to the school rink and practice. "I was a year older," Phil says, "so I got to be the shooter." Appropriately enough, Tony is now the Vezina Trophy goalie of the Chicago Black Hawks.

Though he's lost his temper on the ice more than once, Phil is normally a happy-go-lucky, wisecracking fellow. Yet he's totally serious about hockey. Bobby Orr, in fact, credits Esposito's spirit with being the "main force" that turned the Bruins into a championship team, winner of two Stanley Cups since 1969. "The minute Phil got here," Orr says, "he changed this whole team. He went around training camp bringing us together. He'd say: 'Come on, guys. I know we can make the playoffs, but we've got to stick together.'"

As another indication that Phil really cares, he is highly superstitious, wears a medal stitched inside his thigh pad, keeps a four-leaf clover over his locker, always puts his left shin pad and left skate on first and quickly uncrosses any bad-luck crossed hockey sticks he sees.

As well as he's done in the regular season, Esposito has had his ups and downs in the Stanley Cup playoffs. Against the Canadiens in 1970 he did not have a particularly good series. Boston lost and Esposito said that he was "angry at himself. The Canadiens deserved to win...we didn't." Against the Rangers in 1971-72, he played well, was credited with 7 assists in the five game series. But he was frustrated at taking 41 shots at the goal and not being able to put one in.

His best Stanley Cup performance came against the New York Rangers and the Chicago Black Hawks in 1969. In six games against New York, he scored six goals, in four against Chicago he put in five. That put him within one goal of the record of 12, set by the Montreal Canadiens' Maurice Richard (in nine games) in 1944, and equalled by the Canadiens' Jean Beliveau (in 10 games) in 1956.

Having done so well against his goalie brother, Phil has been heard to say that he is the only one who knows how to beat Tony consistently. He may be kidding. But more and more, it's beginning to look like Phil Esposito has the secret for beating every goalie in the league.

■

Jacques Plante

"Goalkeepers are different from other hockey players," said Toe Blake, former coach of the Montreal Canadiens. Blake was speaking of Jacques Plante, his own goalie at the time, and he might have added that Plante is different from other goalies as well. But Blake's point was well taken. Goalies *are* different, because goal tending is a very special occupation—a dangerous and nerve-wracking one that requires an exceptional combination of eye and body coordination, quick thinking and quick reflexes, steadiness, judgment and an unlimited capacity to perform well under pressure.

Jacques Plante, who, at 43, will begin his seventeenth season as an NHL goalie in the fall of 1972—an amazing record of longevity—is one of the best goalies ever to have played the game. The Vezina Trophy is awarded to the team whose goalie allows the least number of goals in a season, and Plante has won it a record seven times in all and five times in succession.

Plante has remained in action for so long because of his skill in the net, and over the years he has come up with a number of innovations in the art of goaltending, almost all of which have become standard procedure for other goalies in the league. For example, goalies never used to leave the cage. Plante changed that when he came into the NHL in the early 1950's, playing for the Canadiens. His theory was that under the right circumstances and exercising the proper care, there was no reason why a goalie couldn't skate over to a loose puck. A fast skater, Plante went as far as the blue line, some sixty feet from the net, to clear the puck for his defensemen. Plante also came out of the goal to trap the puck when it was behind the cage.

Fans watched in suspense as Plante skated away from the net. Critics said he was "showboating," that there was no point, only great risk, to coming out of the cage. But Dick Irvin, then the Canadiens' coach, backed up his goalie. "Mark my words," Irvin said, "This fellow is going to revolutionize goalkeeping."

That was true, and the most revolutionary move Plante made was to start wearing a face mask. To understand the significance of this, it is necessary to reflect a moment on what a goalie actually does. The cage he guards is a white-netted affair, four feet high and six feet wide. Standing in front of it, holding his wide-bladed stick, the goalie wears 40 pounds of equipment. On his free, "catching" hand is a mitt similar to a first baseman's.

The reason for all this armor is the puck, a frozen, hard-rubber disc, one inch thick and three inches in diameter, weighing six ounces, which opposing players send screaming at the goalie. Pucks frequently blast in at a goalie at speeds of better than 100 miles an hour.

The goalie's job, of course, is to stop the puck—with his mitt, stick or, if necessary, his body. Since a goalie's head is in the line of fire as well, from time to time, the puck can smash sickeningly into a goalie's face.

Plante did not decide to wear a mask overnight. He began to wear a welder's mask for practice sessions in 1955 after his cheek and nose were fractured. In 1958, he was hit in the forehead by a puck during the Stanley Cup playoffs and was then approached by a Fiberglas salesman who suggested that the company could make a mask for him.

After a good bit of experimenting, a satisfactory model was produced, and Plante began to wear it in exhibition games and practice sessions at the beginning of the 1959 season.

In November, 1959, Plante was hit by a hard shot off the stick of the New York Rangers' Andy Bathgate. It took seven stitches to close the three-inch cut, and when Plante came back on the ice in twenty minutes, he had his mask on—for good.

In his years with Montreal, Plante played on strong teams, with stars such as Jean Beliveau, Henri Richard, Boom-Boom Geoffrion and Doug Harvey. Beginning in 1955-56, the Canadiens won five straight Stanley Cups. By the end of the 1959-60 season, Plante had the best statistics of any goalie then playing—an average of 2.11 goals

Plante, top Vezina trophy winner, was first goalie in NHL to wear a mask.

allowed per regular season game, compared to 2.34 for Terry Sawchuck of the Detroit Red Wings.

But Plante did things to annoy his teammates, fans and club officials. He liked to shout instructions to the players, he kissed the ice after a Canadiens' victory, he raised his hands high in a victory sign when the Canadiens came out on top in a game, and this kind of flamboyance on the ice annoyed many. Perhaps because of his behavior, his role in the Canadiens' success was frequently down-graded. But the statistics backed him up, and so did coach Toe Blake, who said: "The goalkeeper has got to be the key man in the organization when you win five Stanley Cups."

Plante's statistics since 1960 also reinforce the conclusion that he is one of the all-time great goalies. Traded to the Rangers in 1963, to St. Louis in 1968 and to Toronto in 1970 (he retired for three years from 1965 to 1968), Plante has maintained his stinginess behind the net. At the end of the 1970-71 season, his lifetime average for goals allowed in regular season games was 2.34. And in more than 100 playoff games, he bettered this figure with a 2.09 average.

Called "Jake-the-Snake," because of his quickness in spearing pucks with his mitt, Plante is a classic stand-up type of goalie who moves out to meet a shooter coming in, trying to cut down his angle. He was born in Quebec province in 1929, began playing hockey when he was three and, amazingly enough, advanced through Canada's minor leagues as a goalie despite being unable to turn his left palm outward, the result of an improperly set break when he was five. He couldn't catch the puck with his left hand and blocked shots on that side with his body. An operation fixed the defect and Plante came up to the Canadiens in 1952.

These days, his life as a goalie is a lot easier, since NHL clubs all carry two goalies who alternate with each other. That has undoubtedly helped Plante to play for so long. But, at the same time, Plante has maintained the high level of his play. In 1970-71, his 1.88 average was the best in the league. In 1971-72, he went up to 2.62, but he was selected for the second All-Star team, and he's under contract to the Maple Leafs for two more years.

Whatever hard knocks he's taken, Plante still enjoys being a goalie. Not long ago, asked if he'd want his son to be a goaltender, Plante said: "Definitely. There's no other place."

Lem Barney

"When you get burned," says Lem Barney, the left cornerback for the Detroit Lions, "you get the lonesomest feeling in the world. You gamble and the whole world sees you. There's no place for a cornerback to hide."

"Burned" is the cornerback's word for what happens when a receiver breaks away from a defensive back to catch a pass for a touchdown. In his six years as one of the game's top defensive backs, Lem Barney has had his share of "lonesomest" moments, as any cornerback must. Even so, Barney is probably the most talented defensive back in the league today, and he's often compared to the legendary "Night Train" Lane, rated tops when he played for Detroit in the 1960's.

Barney gets burned, as good as he is, because the cornerback position is so difficult to play. A cornerback has to be able to run fast and tackle surely. He has to help guard against end sweeps and screen passes. And he has to stop the "bomb." This is difficult to begin with because the receivers he's guarding are sometimes taller and faster than he is and have developed dazzling fakes and moves to befuddle him. It becomes even tougher because the receiver knows exactly what he's going to do, what spot on the field he's heading for and how he intends to get there. The cornerback has to figure out these things for himself.

Under the circumstances, it's not surprising that a lot of bombs are completed, a lot of cornerbacks burned, in the course of a long pro season. After all, cornerbacks these days are guarding receivers like Bob Hayes and Lance Alworth, Paul Warfield and Gene Washington, all of whom qualify as the star of any defensive back's nightmare.

Barney likes to challenge the best. Playing cornerback is, he says, "like any other job. You learn it, you study it, you go at it hard and if you have the ability, you shouldn't have to worry."

There's no doubt of Barney's ability. In the eyes of many observers, in fact, he is the best natural athlete in pro football. Alex Karras, the former tackle for the Lions, is on record as having said that Barney is "the greatest football player in the country."

That may be overstating the case, but certainly Barney is a fantastically gifted performer, fast (100 yards in 9.6), quick-thinking, an elusive runner who's probably the best offensive back playing defense.

Lemuel Joseph Barney, Jr., came up to the Lions in 1967, a 22-year-old from Gulfport, Mississippi who'd played outstanding college football at Jackson State. Barney was in the nature of an "unknown" when Detroit picked him number two in the draft, although he'd averaged over 41 yards as a kicker and intercepted 26 passes in three seasons, 11 in his senior year, and made All-Conference three years running. When someone asked Lions' coach Joe Schmidt what Barney's chances were of becoming a starter in his first season, Schmidt replied: "Pretty darn slight. That's one of the toughest spots in football to play. It takes time to learn, a little longer than other positions. There aren't too many who come in their first year and play it."

Barney was one of the few. He broke right into the starting line-up and proceeded to have a fantastic season. In his first game, he made a spectacular interception of a Bart Starr pass and raced 24 yards into the end zone.

"I was looking for an up-pattern, you know, straight up the field," Barney said after the game. "They're known for throwing the bomb when they're pushed back and want to surprise you. The receiver, Elijah Pitts, went out and I dived and rolled over and ran with the ball. I didn't even know for sure if I was running in the right direction."

He picked up his second TD against Atlanta in the Lions next game. The Atlanta quarterback, Tommy Nofsinger, tried to outguess Barney with a short pass to veteran end Tommy McDonald. Barney read the play, flicked in front of the receiver on the Atlanta 45 and at less than top speed cruised over the goal line.

"I didn't see anybody, so I didn't think there was any use burning up any energy," Barney said later. Pretty cool for a rookie.

Barney went on to lead the NFL in interceptions with 10 (good for 232 yards) and tie an NFL record by returning three of these for touchdowns. He also returned punts for another 100 yards and did the Lions punting, averaging 40 yards a kick. The Lions named him their most valuable defensive player and he made all-pro, an extremely rare honor for a rookie.

From that high point, Barney has continued to play brilliantly. He's made all-pro every year he's been in the league except 1971, when he had an off-year with just three interceptions. On interceptions, punts, kick-off and field goal attempt returns, he's gained more than 2500 yards and scored 11 touchdowns. In 1969, he played with a broken wrist protected by a cast and still registered eight interceptions.

Perhaps Barney's greatest afternoon in pro foot-

ball came in a game at the end of the 1970 season, in which Detroit beat the Packers 20-0. Detroit's victory gave it the right to meet the Dallas Cowboys in a Conference play-off game the following week. The Lions won mainly because Barney ran wild.

At the start of the second half he returned the Packers' kick-off 74 yards, after which Detroit put a field goal on the scoreboard. That was the only score until the fourth quarter, when Donnie Anderson of the Packers punted and Barney zipped the kick back 65 yards to the Lions 13. A 13-yard pass from Greg Landry to Charlie Sanders and the point-after gave Detroit seven more points.

On the very next series of plays, after Detroit had kicked off, Bart Starr flipped a pass in Barney's direction, intended for Packer end Carroll Dale. Barney grabbed the ball and started off. He moved into high gear up one sideline, then cut across the field to the other, faked three Packers out of their cleats and charged into the end zone. It was a 49-yard run, though Barney probably covered double that amount dancing out of the reach of Green Bay tacklers.

That maneuver put the game on ice. In all, Barney registered 233 yards in his afternoon's work.

After the game, Joe Schmidt said: "Barney has an uncanny sense of when to cut. He's the best natural athlete on this club. If I had two others like him, I'd play one next to him and use the other on offense."

Barney finished the 1970 season second in the NFC in interceptions with seven, third in punt returns with a 10 yard average and had two 48-yard kick-off returns.

Barney, whose teammates call him "Stroller" because he is anything but that on a football field, loves the challenge of taking on a receiver and stealing the ball from him. He loves to gamble that he will guess right and not get burned. Though he had three touchdowns scored against his coverage in 1971, he has, during most of his career, won a lot more of his gambles than he's lost. And it's a good bet that Lem Barney will go on gambling— and winning.

As his wife says, "He is cool."

■

Kareem Abdul-Jabbar

It was midway in the fourth quarter of the game that reporters had been calling "the dream game" and "the battle of the century." The Los Angeles Lakers had been behind for most of the game. With nine seconds left in the third period, the Lakers were trailing the Milwaukee Bucks 84-75. Then the Lakers got hot, and with just under seven minutes left in the fourth quarter, they pulled to within two points of Milwaukee, 94-92.

On the floor, Kareem Abdul-Jabbar, formerly known as Lew Alcindor, at least 7'4" of long, lean basketball player, stationed himself near the basket. Guarding him was Wilt Chamberlain, the Laker's large center, at 7' giving away inches to Abdul-Jabbar. Almost glued to each other, the two men bumped and touched again, jockeying for position. The meeting of these two giants was one reason this game in the Milwaukee Arena was receiving so much attention. But their meeting was outweighed by the major reason for the game's drama and significance. That reason was the Los Angeles Lakers' winning streak of 33 straight games, the longest winning streak ever put together in professional sports — not just basketball, but every sport.

Now Milwaukee's Oscar Robertson had the ball. He dribbled forward smoothly, then flicked a pass to Abdul-Jabbar. Abdul-Jabbar pressed against Chamberlain, edged in toward the basket, whirled, leaping high, and dunked a shot. It missed, caromed off the rim. Abdul-Jabbar jumped high again and tipped the shot into the basket.

With that two-pointer, the Bucks went on a tear, tallying 18 points in four minutes while Los Angeles got just two. Abdul-Jabbar put in three more baskets and grabbed four rebounds in the space of two minutes, then left the game to a roaring ovation.

The final score was 120-104. The Bucks had broken the Lakers' fantastic win streak, and the "main man" in the victory was Kareem. He scored 39 points and pulled down 20 rebounds, while Wilt had 15 points and 12 rebounds. Abdul-Jabbar hit from close and from outside, he controlled the boards and boxed Chamberlain out of plays. "I've never seen Jabbar so fired up," said Bill Sharman, the Lakers' coach, after the game. Abdul-Jabbar felt that the victory was a good one because, he said, "They are our toughest competition in the league and it gives us a sense of accomplishment in beating them."

The comment was typical of Abdul-Jabbar, who at 24 will start his third season in the NBA in the fall of 1972. Accomplishment is a major thing for Kareem Abdul-Jabbar, and there are few basketball observers who do not believe that this tall young man will dominate the NBA for the next decade or more. He is, quite simply, a fantastic ballplayer who combines his height with exceptional coordination and quickness and fantastic moves. Jerry Lucas of the New York Knicks believes, along with many others, that Abdul-Jabbar is the best center who has ever played the game. Shooting right or left-handed, facing the hoop or away from it, Abdul-Jabbar has a variety of shots so dazzling they would present a problem to a defender if Kareem were a foot shorter. At his height, he takes on the aspect of being unbeatable. And he's still learning, still sharpening his natural talents. "I knew I would have no trouble being a competant professional," he has said, "but I want to be *excellent.*"

As Lew Alcindor, he started being excellent when he was a schoolboy at Power Memorial High School in New York. When he entered as a freshman, he was already 6' 10" tall, but what was exciting about him as a basketball player was that, unlike many very tall men, he had exceptional coordination. He led Power to a 71-game winning streak.

In college, at the University of California in Los Angeles (UCLA), he was equally devastating, and

Jabbar has small man's grace, quick moves.

be pushed around by beefier centers in the league.

Abdul-Jabbar's second year was nothing less than fabulous. When the season was over, he had poured in 2596 points, averaging 31.7 per game. He also averaged 16 rebounds. He led the Bucks to their first NBA title and was named the league's Most Valuable Player. During the regular season, the Bucks won 66 of 82 games, and in the playoff finals they ran through the Baltimore Bullets in four straight games, the first time this ever happened.

Throughout the season, and in the playoffs as well, Abdul-Jabbar proved conclusively that he had come of age as a basketball player. Against Baltimore for the championship, he had the Bullets handcuffed not only by the positive things he did, his passing, shooting and rebounding. But simply by being in the game he made them change their whole attack. A running and driving team, Baltimore was forced to shoot from outside instead of trying for layups because Abdul-Jabbar's presence made driving in so difficult. Baltimore forward Jack Marin said: "You look up there and see him by the rim, and its like taking a golf shot through a tree; it's supposed to be 90 per cent air but you always hit a twig."

And the Bullets' Kevin Loughery said: "He may only block a shot here or there, but guys have to change their shots because of him. He's the greatest defensive player I've seen since Bill Russell."

That was his defensive contribution. On offense, closely guarded by Baltimore's Wes Unseld, he still put in an average of 25 points a game.

In 1971-72, Jabbar and the Bucks did not quite come up to the level of their play in the previous season. And contrary to the showdown meeting that broke the Lakers' 33-game winning streak, things went in Wilt's favor when the two teams met in the playoffs. He was able to keep Alcindor under a lot more control, and the Lakers took the series and went on to beat the New York Knicks in the finals.

But Kareem Abdul-Jabbar will be back, and there will be more championships for the Milwaukee Bucks. Because Abdul-Jabbar doesn't like to lose. "I've been winning for many years," he says," and I believe in it. With me losing is an exception, and that's the way I want to keep it."

in his sophomore year, despite a ruling, obviously aimed at him, that made "dunking" illegal, UCLA won the national championship. They went on to win two more championships—and in Abdul-Jabbar's senior year they lost just one game.

He signed with the Bucks after the 1968-69 season for a reported $1.4 million. The speculation that then occurred was not over whether he would be good as a pro, but over how good he would be. The verdict is now in: very good, perhaps the best ever to play the game.

In his first year, he averaged 28.8 points a game and was third in the league in rebounding with an average of 14.5.

And right from the start, he worked hard to perfect his game. He developed a hook shot, improved his passing, became a lot more mobile. And he put on weight, getting up to 250 pounds, so that he was no longer the skinny kid who could easily

Johnny Unitas

Johnny U—"the old master." He's 39 now and after 16 seasons there aren't too many left. But the familiar, angular figure still trots out, number 19 on the blue and white jersey, wearing the incongruous black, over-the-ankle football shoes (shades of "Broadway Joe") that send an instant message: Johnny Unitas has been playing this game since 1956.

Before the 1971 season began, they said this might be the year he'd have to bow out. In the spring, he ruptured an Achilles tendon playing paddleball. That injury heals slowly in an old man, they said. He'd been bothered by a "tennis elbow," too, over the past few seasons—torn muscles on the inside of the elbow that came from all those passes thrown.

Close to 5000 attempts, more than half completed. Close to 300 touchdown passes. Pushing 40,000 yards gained passing. Statistics that remind one of the Grand Canyon being formed, water eating into rock over ages of time. No one else has ever gained 40,000 yards passing. His closest competitor is Sonny Jurgensen of the Washington Redskins, also going into his sixteenth year, but some 10,000 yards behind Unitas.

Over the years, there have been plenty of injuries—torn cartilage, broken ribs, punctured lungs. He came back from them. And in 1971, the ruptured Achilles tendon healed, he came back again. He didn't take the Colts all the way to a repeat of Super Bowl number V in 1970, when Baltimore beat the Dallas Cowboys 16-13. But he came close.

He had his good days and his bad ones. On his good ones, he was very good (though he can't throw as long as he used to), cutting open opposing defenses like a skillful surgeon.

Against the Miami Dolphins, for example, in the team's second meeting of the season in Baltimore early in December, he engineered a 14-3 victory that gave the Colts first place in the American Football Conference's eastern division.

Unitas has said that he believes his greatest strength as a quarterback lies in his "knowledge of defenses and ability to adjust to them." He has also said: "You take what they give you. They've got to give you something. All you have to do is find out what it is."

Facing the zone defense thrown up by Miami, Unitas proved the accuracy of these comments. In the first half, he controlled the game like a puppet master, pulling the strings of perfect calls that resulted in two long, beautifully-sustained touchdown drives. With the Miami linebackers and defensive backs dropping back to shut off the longer pass, Unitas began to throw to his backs coming out of the backfield, alternating these passes with running plays that probed holes in the Dolphins' three-man line. When Miami began to guard against passes and runs on the outside, Unitas sent his backs into the middle of the line.

There were no spectacular long gainers, no "bombs," but instead, a steady, successful series of first downs. When the half ended, the score was 14-0 Baltimore. Colts' back Tom Matte scored both touchdowns, on seven-yard and one-yard runs. But Unitas completed 12 of 13 passes for 103 yards. The two touchdown drives covered 81 and 87 yards in 34 plays and ate up close to 20 minutes on the clock. In the second half, Baltimore's defense smothered the Dolphins.

"Unitas did everything right," Miami coach Don Shula said after the game. Nick Buoniconti, the Dolphins' middle linebacker, and rated one of the best, had a frustrating afternoon. Unitas took particular care to run plays away from him. "You don't expect the quarterback to be reading you like that," Buoniconti said later. "A quarterback usually looks at the strong safety and strong side linebacker for his keys. But with Unitas it's scary. He seems to know what you're going to do before you do."

Unitas had another good day in the American Conference playoff against the Cleveland Browns a month later as the Colts won 20-3. He completed 13 of 21 passes for 143 yards, and again calling plays with marvelous precision, sent running backs Matte and Don Nottingham on successful forays into the Cleveland line. But the string ran out for the Colts when they played Miami again for the American Conference title and the right to go against Dallas in the Super Bowl. Quarterback Bob Griese of the Dolphins picked apart the Colt defense with the precision of a Unitas, and the Colts were never able to get a sustained attack going as Miami won 21-0.

Victory and defeat have come to Unitas in turn over the years of his career, and one of his strengths has been the ability to put defeat out of his mind and move on to the game or season ahead. "Of course I'm not happy to lose," he says. "Sure I'm upset. But it happened, so it happened."

The confidence reflected by that remark is a strong part of Johnny Unitas' makeup. He grew up in Pittsburgh, played quarterback for St. Justin High School, dreamed of going to Notre Dame and of playing professional football. Notre Dame rejected his bid for a scholarship because, a coach said, at his high school weight of 135 he was too small to play college football. He went to the University of Louisville instead, gained 50 pounds and starred at quarterback.

He was drafted by the Pittsburgh Steelers after college but cut from the squad before the season began. Still, he says, he was confident that somehow he'd get into the pro ranks. For a year, he worked for a construction company and played "sandlot" football at $6 a game. Then a call came from the Baltimore Colts, who needed a back-up quarterback.

As it turned out, halfway through the season, the Colts' first-string quarterback, George Shaw, was injured in a game against the Chicago Bears. Unitas came in with the Colts leading 21-20. When the game was over, the score was 56-21 in favor of the Bears. Unitas had fumbled three times and the Bears turned these mistakes and an intercepted pass into four touchdowns.

But Unitas came back to do the job for the Colts the rest of that season. And he started a record that may never be equalled, throwing a touchdown pass in 47 straight games. The first game was in December, 1956, and Unitas was not stopped until five years later, when the Los Angeles Rams shut him out in December, 1960.

In 1957, Unitas was installed as the team's first-string quarterback and led the league in passing yardage and touchdown passes as the Colts won the NFL championship. He was named the most valuable player in the title game and was voted the Jim Thorpe Trophy as the NFL's most outstanding player.

Against the New York Giants in the title game, Unitas demonstrated his fantastic ability to function well under the most extreme pressure—in other words, his confidence. With the Colts behind 17-13, just two minutes left in the game and most of the 60,000 fans in Yankee Stadium screaming for a Giant victory, Unitas took the Colts from their own 14 to the Giant 13-yard line. A field goal tied the score.

Now the teams were in a sudden-death overtime. Unitas brought the Colts down the field. Inside the Giants' 10-yard line, against coach Weeb Ewbank's orders, Unitas threw a pass to the one-yard line, then sent fullback Alan Ameche in for a touchdown and Colt victory, 23-17. Asked later why he had risked the pass, he said: "When you know what you're doing, they're not intercepted."

Over the years, in good seasons and poor ones, Unitas has displayed the same confidence. He believes a quarterback should call his own plays. "I have to do what I think is right," he says. "I'm the one out on the field. If the coach doesn't like the plays I call, he has another quarterback sitting right there on the bench."

Unitas' teammates go along with his judgment all the way. As one of them, guard Glenn Ressler said recently: "You just believe that if there is anybody who can call a play that's certain to work, it's him."

Brooks Robinson

It is the sixth inning of the first game of the 1970 World Series between the Baltimore Orioles and the Cincinnati Reds. Lee May of the Reds is at bat. He swings and sends a hard-hit ball down the third base line. The ball skips past the bag, heading out into left field for what will surely be a double.

But the Orioles' third baseman, Brooks Robinson, intercepts the ball somehow, his glove outstretched to snare it backhanded. Almost in the same instant he throws it over his shoulder toward first base. The ball reaches Boog Powell on one hop—in time to retire May by a split second. An incredible play.

The Reds get a walk and a hit after this, so Robinson's play saves a run. The final score is 4-3, in favor of the Orioles. Robinson hits the game-winning homer in the eighth inning.

The next day, Robinson does it again: with one out and a man on first, May again hits a hot shot down the third base line, Robinson again spears the ball backhanded. He fires it to second to start a double play. The Orioles win 6-5 and Cincinnati manager Sparky Anderson says: "If I threw a sandwich out on the field, that guy at third would turn it into a double play." The Reds are beginning to see what this series is all about. It is Brooks Robinson versus Cincinnati, and Robinson is not about to come out second best.

Third game. First two Cincinnati batters get on base. Tony Perez comes up. He hits a bullet down the third base line. Robinson spears it neatly and starts a rally-choking double play. Johnny Bench follows with a missile-shot liner to Robinson's left. Robinson launches himself in a horizontal dive and catches the ball before it hits the ground. It is only the best catch anyone has ever seen.

Now the Reds know for sure. There's not much point trying to outplay Robinson, but they take a crack at it anyhow. They manage to win the fourth

game from him, but he comes back strong to take the fifth, mercifully ending the unequal contest.

Immediately after the game, Robinson's glove is mailed off to Baseball's Hall of Fame in Cooperstown, New York, to be permanently exhibited, and someone suggests that the car awarded to Robinson by *Sport* magazine be given to his glove instead. But would that be fair to his bat, which stroked nine hits, including two homers, and six runs batted in, for a .428 average?

Brooks Robinson's exploits in the '70 Series had fans all over the country gasping in delight and amazement. Baltimore fans were not as surprised. They've been watching Robinson make amazing plays and bang out clutch hits for years, which is why Robinson is the most popular man in that city. Robinson came up to the Baltimore team as an 18-year-old rookie at the end of the 1955 season, and after a couple of more trips back to the minors, took over third base for the Orioles in 1957.

Robinson got to the Orioles after just one year in Class B ball. Before that, he'd played in junior high school in Little Rock, Arkansas, where he was born, and for the Little Rock Boys Club, since his high school didn't have a team. He started out as a second baseman, and was switched to third during his first minor league season because, in his manager's judgment, he was too slow to cover second.

In fact, following the scout's traditional judgment that the two things to look for in a young ballplayer are speed of foot and a good arm, Robinson was not an outstanding prospect. His junior high coach says: "He couldn't run a lick. He had good, quick hands but he didn't look like he'd ever be much of a hitter." The coach noted one impressive thing about him, however: "He'd always do something to help you win."

His minor league coach, George Staller, now

Robinson wins games in field and at bat.

the Orioles' first base coach, reported in 1955 that Robinson was "adequate" as a second baseman, but would make a "great" third baseman because he had agility and quick hands. And by 1958, general manager Paul Richards was convinced that Robinson was going to be a star.

Robinson has indeed become more than a "star." He has always had weaknesses as a hitter: he swings at too many bad pitches, particularly high fast balls. His lifetime average is .274, respectable but far from brilliant, though he has hit more homers than any other third baseman ever did. But he makes his hits count. In 1969, for example, though he batted just .234, he drove home 84 runs. As one sportswriter said, "He bats .276 on the average and .476 in the clutch."

It is on the field that he is truly brilliant, of course. He's won the Golden Glove award as the American League's best-fielding third baseman for the last 12 years. And he's done it not just by handling easy chances, but by consistently making the fantastic plays he made in the series against Baltimore. He is, in fact, in the judgment of many experts, the best third baseman in the history of the game.

Robinson is admired for his coolness in a game, and perhaps this quality accounts for his effectiveness in clutch situations. What lies behind it is confidence, control and discipline, a certain rational approach to the game that has enabled Robinson to get the most from his talent. A couple of seasons ago, when his hitting fell off, he decided to use a lighter bat and to hit to right field more often instead of trying to pull the ball to left. The prescription worked and his hitting picked up.

He's applied the same analytical approach to his fielding, and he's constantly looking for ways to improve his capacity to make a given play. For example, he concluded a number of years ago that there was a flaw in the way he was going to his right to field balls backhanded. His gloved hand was blocking his view when he had to throw. The solution was to get his gloved hand way out across his body before he was in position to catch the ball.

Still, Robinson doesn't feel there are too many things you can teach a young player about fielding. He believes the key thing to remember in fielding is to keep the glove down low; most balls that fielders miss, he points out, go under rather than over their glove. He's one of the best in making a barehanded pickup and getting off a quick throw on a bunt. The most important point to remember in making this play, he thinks, is always to come in and field the ball with the left foot forward, which lets you get off the throw in the same motion you use to pick up the ball. In the end, though, he believes that experience and watching good players closely are the best ways for a young player to improve his fielding.

Brooks Robinson is, by unanimous vote, one of the nicest and kindest men in sports, and during the off-season he makes himself available for charitable and civic events in Baltimore, where he lives, and elsewhere, with gracious generosity. Because he's universally liked and esteemed, there was general approval when he received the second annual Commissioner's Award as "The player who best typifies the game of baseball on and off the field." (The first winner was Willie Mays.)

How well Robinson represents the game of baseball at its best on the field is revealed in a comment made by Johnny Bench after the 1970 World Series. "I couldn't even get angry with Brooks at what he was doing to us. I just walked back to the dugout appreciating what his plays were — things of beauty."

Gene Washington

There's no doubt about it, Gene Washington, the San Francisco 49ers young wide receiver, has a few fans. For example, Jim Shofner, the 49ers defensive backfield coach. "If I were playing against Gene," Shofner says, "I would hold him or push him. There just isn't any legal way one man can stop him." And Stanford football coach John Ralston: "Gene's simply fantastic when it comes to catching a pass. He's the best I've seen at it." And John Brodie: "Gene is going away the best in the league. If he has any weaknesses I don't know what they are." and Al Bresler, who starred in college at Auburn and came to the 49ers spring training camp in 1971: "He has to be king of the hill. There's no way anybody can be shiftier, faster or more sure-handed. The moves he makes have to be seen to be believed."

Maybe Bresler, never having played pro ball, was over-impressed? Maybe, but during practice sessions for the January 1971 Pro Bowl, the top performers in the league watched with particular attention every time Washington ran a pass pattern. The conclusion seems certain: Gene Washington is something special.

A relaxed and likeable yet highly disciplined 25-year-old, Gene Alden Washington has created this kind of attention after just three seasons in the pro ranks. But they were hardly ordinary ones. In his first year, 1969, Washington caught 51 passes for 711 yards and three TD's to rank tenth in the NFL in number of receptions. In 1970 he ran wild, grabbing 53 passes for 1100 yards and 12 TD's, which put him first in yardage in the NFL and

made him a unanimous all-pro selection. Facing double coverage almost every time he ran a pattern in 1971, he still caught 46 passes for 884 yards and four TD's to lead the NFC in yardage.

Washington's success as a pro is no surprise to West Coast fans who've followed his career in high school and college. Born in Alabama, Washington grew up in Long Beach, California. At Polytechnic High School in Long Beach, he was a three sport man, playing football, basketball and baseball. He also maintained an A-minus scholastic average and was president of the integrated school.

At graduation he had offers from 50 schools and chose Stanford because of its academic excellence. Playing quarterback, he led the Stanford freshmen to an unbeaten season in 1965 and there was speculation that he might become the first black quarterback in pro football. But four games into the season in 1966, he hurt his shoulder and when he came back in 1967, he chose to play end instead.

Washington is probably one of the better-adjusted athletes around and nothing if not a realist. "I knew I couldn't throw well enough to be a pro quarterback," he says now. "The injury was just another reason for the change. I wanted to play pro ball and I wanted to be drafted in the first round instead of the eighteenth. I figured I would be drafted as a defensive back or a flanker. I thought I might as well utilize the talents I had." And then he adds, "Besides, I felt, and still feel, that at the time, there wasn't any place for a black quarterback. It still seems that way, but it might change in a couple of years."

In any event, as a wide receiver he proceeded to tear up the Pacific-8 Conference. In 1967 he caught 46 passes. In 1968, his senior year, he ranked fourth in the country in pass receiving, with 71 catches for 1117 yards and eight touchdowns. He made All-Conference, was mentioned on several All-America teams and was named the outstanding offensive player in the East-West game.

With all of his natural talent, Washington is still anxious to learn. As his college coach, John Ralston said of him, "He's a wonderful all-around guy who makes coaching a delight. He has a consuming passion to excel." One thing Washington has learned to excel in is blocking. At a lithe and muscular 6'1" and 190 pounds, he should be at a disadvantage hitting much bigger linebackers, but he's turned out to be one of the better blocking ends in the league. "I didn't know how to block at all when I came up to the 49ers," he admits. "At training camp, Ernie Zwahlen, our offensive line coach, drilled us in blocking technique. It turned out I like to block. It's fun."

Washington has the same "there's a lot I can learn" attitude toward pass catching. After his great season in 1970, he said: "I was happy with my year but I didn't think I reached my limit. I made all-pro but I can still improve on my pass patterns. If you run a pattern the way it's meant to be run, you should get open every time."

Washington feels that his experience playing quarterback has been a big help to him as a pass receiver. "I know how the quarterback thinks," Gene says. "I know how much time he has to unload the ball. A guy running downfield may think he's open, but from the quarterback's view he's not." Washington's feeling is confirmed by defensive backfield coach Jim Shofner. "Washington can relate to Brodie," Shofner says. "He doesn't just run patterns, he looks to see what will work and tells John."

Shofner thinks that Washington's greatest asset as a receiver is body control. "There are lots of receivers who are fast," Shofner says. "Bob Hayes and guys like that. But Gene can run at maximum speed and still be under control. He can make his moves without slowing down."

Head fake, eye feint, half step, dropped shoulder —these are some of the tricks of the receiving trade and Washington uses them as well as any end in the league to accomplish the receiver's goal—getting free. Otis Taylor, Kansas City's great end, has a high regard for Washington's capacity to lose a defender. "He gets free in unusual situations," Taylor says. Washington himself thinks that the toughest pattern to run is the corner pattern and he admires the way Fred Biletnikoff, the NFL's top receiver in 1971, runs it.

On his best days, Washington has been superlative. In an exhibition game in 1971, he caught two touchdown passes against Cleveland. The first one was for 50 yards and Washington grabbed it after faking veteran defensive back Erich Barnes out of position. His second TD went for 46 yards and Washington leaped high to snare the ball in a one-on-one scramble with Clarence Scott. That catch brought an expression of amazement from Cleveland coach Nick Skorich, who's seen a few catches in his time. "Scott tipped the ball," Skorich said later, "but when it came down, Washington had it in one hand and Scott's watch in the other." In other words, inspired larceny.

In 1970, Washington had any number of great afternoons, catching five passes for 119 yards against the Bears, seven for 145 yards against the Rams and five for 131 yards and three touchdowns against the New Orleans Saints.

Like every other player in the league, Washington would like to see his team in the Super Bowl, and in 1971, San Francisco made a strong try, finally losing to the Dallas Cowboys 24-3 in a game in which they never overcame the disadvantage of an early Dallas touchdown. On the way to that meeting, San Francisco played well. One of their most important victories came over the Washington Redskins, coached by former LA Rams coach George Allen. The 49ers won, 24-20, and the decisive points came on a 78-yard pass to Washington which made the score 19-3. Washington outran the Redskin defender to gather the ball in on the Redskin 40-yard line and jetted down to the goal line.

"I was surprised that they only had single coverage on Gene on that one," John Brodie said after the game. The way Gene Washington catches a football, there won't be too many days when that's true.

Johnny Bench

When Johnny Bench was 17 years old and playing for Tampa in the Florida State League, Yogi Berra looked him over and said: "He can do it all now." Three years later, in the middle of his rookie year with the Cincinnati Reds, Bench got an autographed baseball from Ted Williams, the game's greatest student of hitting and a hard man to impress. "A Hall of Famer for sure," Williams wrote on the ball.

In that rookie year of 1968, Bench batted .275, hit 15 home runs, and drove in 82 runs. He also set a major league record for the greatest number of games caught by a rookie, 154. And won the Golden Glove as the National League's outstanding defensive receiver—the first rookie to win it. And was Rookie of the Year. Not a bad start in the major leagues.

The following year, 1969, Bench socked 26 home runs and drove in 90 runs, batting .293. Then came 1970, the year that Bench made Ted Williams' prediction look like a sure thing. Leading Cincinnati to its first National League pennant since 1961, Bench hit 45 home runs and batted in 148 runs. Cincinnati's powerful team, the "Big Red Machine," with Pete Rose and Bobby Tolan aiding Bench's bombardment, ran away from the rest of the league. Bench was named Most Valuable Player, at 22 the youngest catcher ever to receive this honor.

Although Cincinnati lost to the Orioles in the World Series, there seemed to be no reason why the team wouldn't come back strong in 1971. Instead, the Reds slumped badly, ending up in third place in the western division. Bench fell from the heights of 1970 to 27 homers, 61 RBIs and a .238 average. None of the Reds had a great year, but perhaps because more was expected of him, Bench took more than his share of the boos. "You try to say that you don't hear it," he said after the season. "I heard it. Boy, I heard it and it hurt."

In 1971, Bench had tried to pull nearly every pitch, went into a slump and then couldn't get his old swing back. In 1972, he reported for 10 days, hitting work in the Florida Instructional League. "I have to get it corrected," he said, "and I'm going to keep at it until I do."

But when the season started, Bench went one for 22, and a month and a half later he was hitting just .246. Hall of Fame talk was fading fast. Then, suddenly, Bench got back his booming bat. In Houston, he smacked two home runs and a bases-loaded single, his second homer winning the game 9-5. Next game Bench hit season's homer number nine. Against the Phillies, he hit a homer in the seventh inning to tie the score 1-1, and in the eighteenth he blasted another with two men on to win the game 6-3. That made it seven homers in five games, which tied a league record set in 1929.

Bench went on to blast pitchers with abandon, and by the end of their road trip, Cincinnati had moved from fourth to first place. Bench had collected 21 hits in 51 at bats, had 18 homers and a .306 average. "Man, I haven't felt so good in two years," Bench said in the middle of the streak.

Coming back strong as a hitter, Johnny Bench backed up the feeling of most baseball men that he's the best catcher in the game, ranking with such all-time greats as Gabby Hartnett, Bill Dickey, Yogi Berra, Josh Gibson and Mickey Cochrane. Good catchers have been rare because catching is perhaps the most difficult job in baseball. It requires physical durability first of all, the strength and desire to survive being hit by foul tips, wild pitches and sliding runners. And there's the strain of squatting down some 200 times a game every day of the season. Catching requires, besides, a good arm to prevent stealing and a good mind to read opposing hitters and handle pitchers.

Bench, as Yogi Berra said, "does it all." His arm is phenomenal, his throws hard and accurate. "He can hit a flea's eyelash at second base," one Cincinnati pitcher has said. He's trained himself always to grab the ball across the seams as he pulls it out of the mitt, so that his throws don't curve or

Bench performed sensationally in 1970, led Cincinnati to its first pennant in thirty years.

fade. He has large hands (he can hold seven base-balls in one hand) and long fingers, which allow him to grip the ball way out at the end and get a whip-like motion when he throws.

Bench catches the ball one-handed, using only his glove. This keeps his right hand away from pitches that might damage it. It also enables him to pull the ball out of the glove with great speed when he sees a man trying to steal or wandering off a base. In addition, he can throw from a crouch as fast and hard as a catcher who has to take the time to stand up, which is why he is so good at picking men off base. The result is that Bench stops oppos-ing runners from running, making it a lot easier for his pitchers to concentrate on pitching.

From behind the plate, Bench is a "take charge" guy. He is continuously urging his teammates to hustle, hollering out encouragement, shouting at fielders to throw to the right base. He handles pitchers brilliantly as well, insists that they follow his signals, babies them or needles them into throw-ing the pitch he wants them to throw.

Johnny Bench always knew he wanted to play major league baseball. He decided to be a catcher

at the urging of his father. Ted Bench had been a semi-pro catcher, and he reasoned that this position offered the fastest route to the major leagues be-cause there were so few good catchers around. Johnny is one-eighth Choctaw Indian on his father's side—which gives him his high cheekbones. He grew up in Binger, Oklahoma (population 730) and played Little League and high school baseball. In high school, he pitched at times, compiling a 16-1 record, and batted .675.

He was picked up by the Reds in 1965, sent to Tampa, then to Buffalo. In 1967 he had a homer every fourth time he went to bat, was named Minor League Player of the Year and called up to Cincin-nati at the end of that season.

Bench sees the future quite clearly. Now making $85,000, he wants to be the first catcher in base-ball history to be paid $100,000. And he wants to be "the greatest catcher ever to play the game." Back in Binger, when he was in the second grade, his teacher asked him what he wanted to be when he grew up. "They laughed when I said I wanted to be a major league ballplayer," Bench recalls. No one is laughing now.

■

Roberto Clemente

Roberto Clemente can get very angry at times. Before the 1971 World Series, for example, he was furious at the condition of the field in the Baltimore Orioles' Memorial Stadium. Several football games had been played there, and, Clemente said, "There are holes all over. If a ball is hit to me and bounces away, everybody will say Clemente is a bad fielder."

Roberto was also annoyed because reporters gave the Pirates little chance of beating the Orioles. "I'll bet we will win," he shouted at a group of reporters as the Pirates were practicing the day before the first game, "and I don't care if I go to jail for betting."

Clemente was kidding about gambling, but he was very serious about the Pirates winning. For a while, his prediction didn't look too good. The Pirates played badly as they lost the first two games 5-3 and 11-3, though Clemente had four hits in nine times at bat, including two doubles. In all of World Series history, only four teams had ever been able to come back and win after losing the first two games.

The Pirates became the fifth, and Clemente had more to do with their victory than any one else on the field. In the third game, he singled in a run. Then, in a key play, he beat out a hit to the Orioles' pitcher, Mike Cuellar, charging down to first so aggressively that Cuellar pulled Boog Powell off the bag with his throw. A walk and a three run homer by Bob Robertson followed to put the game away for Pittsburgh, 5-1.

In the fourth game, which Pittsburgh won 4-3,

Clemente went three for four, just missing a home run on a whistling drive that the umpire ruled foul. In the fifth game, he weighed in with a single and a run batted in as Nelson Briles pitched a two-hit shutout for a 4-0 Pirate win.

Now Pittsburgh led 3-2 in games and Clemente had banged out nine hits. Back in Baltimore for the sixth game, Clemente did his best to make his prediction come true, slamming a home run and a triple. But Baltimore came back to win 3-2 in the tenth inning.

Clemente had 11 hits now. Two more and he would break the record for number of hits in a seven game Series. He managed just one in the final game as Mike Cuellar and Steve Blass pitched strong games. Cuellar retired the first 11 batters. Clemente came up for his second at bat in the fourth inning and whacked Cuellar's first pitch 400 feet over the center field fence. The Pirates got one more run on Willie Stargell's single and Jose Pagan's double, while Steve Blass held the Orioles to one run. The underdog Bucs, led by Clemente, were the World Champions for 1971.

Clemente hit safely in every game, ended up with 12 hits in 29 at bats, a .414 average. Back in 1960, when the Pirates beat the Yankees, Clemente also hit safely in all seven games, had 9 hits and a .310 average. In 1971, he won the car awarded by *Sport* magazine to the Series' most valuable player. Despite the chewed-up field in Baltimore, despite a sore shoulder, Clemente had come through—as he usually does. "I have peace of mind now," he said after the Series. "Now everyone knows the way Roberto Clemente plays."

Getting the recognition he deserves has always been important to Roberto Walker Clemente, and there is much to be said in support of his feeling that he has been underrated as a ballplayer. Born in Puerto Rico in 1934, Clemente dreamed of a baseball career when he was growing up, and he began playing professional ball in Puerto Rico at 17. He soon attracted major league attention. He was an exceptionally strong hitter and a super fielder with a phenomenal arm.

Signed by the Dodgers, then still in Brooklyn, for a $10,000 bonus, Clemente was sent to their Montreal farm club in 1954. As a bonus player in a minor league, he could be drafted by any other major league team. So the Dodgers tried to conceal their prize from other teams. "If I struck out I stayed in the lineup," Clemente recalls. "If I played well I was benched." But a Pirate scout figured out what was going on, and Pittsburgh drafted him for the larcenously small sum of $4000. In his first five seasons with the Pirates, Clemente averaged .280. His best year was 1956, when he batted .311.

In 1960, as the Pirates took their first pennant in 30 years, Clemente batted .314, drove in 94 runs, had 16 home runs and led National League outfielders in assists. But when the results of the Most Valuable Player balloting became known, Clemente discovered that he had finished eighth. The winner was Pirate shortstop Dick Groat. Clemente was dismayed and angry. He felt that he should have at least finished higher than eighth.

Clemente's anger had immediate results. As Clemente himself has said: "I play better when I am mad." He set out to show the world that a mistake had been made and the following year, 1961, he hit .351 to win his first batting title. In 1964, he won the title again with a .339 average, and in 1965 he did it again with an average of .329. His fourth title came in 1967 when he hit .357, the highest average in the National League since 1948. Only three men, Stan Musial, Rogers Hornsby and Honus Wagner have ever won more National league batting titles than Clemente.

Meanwhile, in 1966, at the urging of Pirates' manager Harry Walker, he became a "power hitter," blasting 29 home runs and batting in 119 runs.

Because of his hitting, the Pirates battled for the pennant down to the last days of the season, and Clemente was named Most Valuable Player.

Clemente accomplished these feats while struggling against a succession of injuries. His back began to bother him soon after he hit the majors. This brought charges that he was "dogging" it, but a subsequent medical examination indicated that he had an out-of-place vertebra. In 1961, he had a painful elbow injury. Over the winter of 1964-65, he came down with malaria and was still weak from it when the season started. In 1966, his back and leg were a problem. In 1968 he injured his shoulder in a fall. In 1970 he hurt his back again. Clemente has been accused of being a hypochondriac. But if he has been highly vocal about his aches and injuries, he has also played in spite of them, sometimes in great pain.

The hypochondriac charge makes Clemente angry, too. It is, he feels, part of the unfair treatment he's received. He believes that he deserves to be ranked with Mays and Aaron and Mantle, ballplayers of his era who've received far more recognition than he has.

And his record supports Clemente's feeling. In 1970, at the age of 36, he hit .345. That season, too, he set a new major league record by getting five hits in each of two consecutive games. In 1971, he hit .352, and capped that with his World Series performance. There is no doubt that Clemente is one of the finest natural hitters in baseball. His lifetime average of .318 is the highest of any active player. At the start of the 1972 season, he was just 118 hits away from the exclusive 3000-hit club.

Defensively, he has been equally outstanding, winning the Golden Glove as the best rightfielder in the league 10 times. He set a major league record for most years leading the league in assists for outfielders — a tribute to his arm, which is rated the most powerful in baseball.

In short, as the Pirates' Bill Mazeroski says, "He's the total ballplayer. A lot of guys are considered superstars when they're just super-hitters."

Brooks Robinson had what will serve as the last word on Roberto Clemente after the 1971 World Series: "You read about him, you hear about him," Robinson said. "But in real life he's even better."